LEARNING TO CELEBRATE

JOSEPH GELINEAU

Learning to Celebrate

THE MASS AND ITS MUSIC
16 SUGGESTED APPROACHES

TRANSLATED BY MARY ANSELM GROVER, SNJM

THE PASTORAL PRESS
WASHINGTON, DC

ISBN: 0-912405-21-X

The Pastoral Press
225 Sheridan Street, NW
Washington, DC 20011
(202) 723-5800

The Pastoral Press is the publications division of the National
Association of Pastoral Musicians, a membership organization
of musicians and clergy dedicated to fostering the art of
musical liturgy.

Cover, book design and type: Paul Gunzelmann
Lincoln Graphics/Washington

Printed in the United States of America

CONTENTS

INTRODUCTION

Joseph Gelineau published his first musical version
of the Psalms in 1954; they were translated into
English in 1956 and have been used as basic
liturgical repertoire ever since. Gelineau has gone
on to writing texts for liturgy, teaching liturgical
studies at Institut Catholique, and serving as musi-
cian and priest at St. Ignace Parish in Paris. He also
serves five rural parishes as their "itinerant" pastor.

Learning to Celebrate, as a commentary on the
General Instruction of the Roman Missal, is deceptively simple. It is simple because it is well organized and provides easy access to the ideas that
Gelineau has about the liturgy. It is deceptively
simple because Gelineau's insights separate what is
important from what is unimportant, disclosing the
key issues for the reader's reflection.

Learning to Celebrate was first published as a series
of articles in *Eglise Qui Chante* and then edited into
a book: *Apprendre a Celebrer: la messe et ses
chants*. The original references to French liturgical
music have been edited for English-speaking
readers.

All of the persons who take on the responsibility of
ministry are encouraged and required to engage in
extensive training, education, and participation for
assuming their roles of minister. The Assembly—
the whole parish—is recognized as the primary
minister, yet adequate training programs for them

have yet to be found. *Learning to Celebrate* is designed precisely to meet this need: a simple, straightforward presentation within reach and understanding of most American parish assemblies.

As the Constitution on the Sacred Liturgy so clearly states: "Pastors must...realize that when the liturgy is celebrated something more is required than the mere observance of the laws governing valid and lawful celebration. It is also their *duty to ensure that the faithful take part fully aware of what they are doing...*" (CSL #11). This book is presented to pastors to help them assume their mandated responsibility.

Rev. Virgil C. Funk

PART I

THE PIVOTAL POINTS
OF THE CELEBRATION

1

COMING TOGETHER

Christians: people who gather together

Acts 2, 1 On Pentecost the disciples of Jesus "had all gathered together." From this assembly the church was born. There is no church (= convening of a group, gathering together) without an assembly.

Significance

Matt. 18, 20 —Here the Risen Lord is present in the midst of his own;

1 Cor. 12–14 —Here the power of the Spirit is manifested through those who act in his name;

Acts 13 —From here those going forth to preach the Gospel take their leave;

Acts 2, 38 —It is here that those seeking Baptism come to make their request;

Romans 12, 1 —It is here believers renew themselves in order to lead a holy, dedicated life.

Practice

—When I come into the assembly, the first sign offered to my faith is the presence of my brothers and sisters; the gentleman on my right and the lady on my left are Christ for me. A greeting or a smile acknowledges this.

Gal. 3, 28 —Among the baptized "there are no more distinctions between Jew and Greek, slave and free, male and female." In a spirit of faith we are invited to overcome differences of race, social standing, sex, age, etc.

—The stranger, the poor, the transient, the newcomer, all have a right to a special welcome; as also the person who still wishes to remain anonymous.

—The absent faithful are also a part of the assembly: those who could not come; those whose rhythm of participation is not on a weekly basis.

The day of assembly is the Lord's Day

Significance

—Christians have a special day for their assembly;

—the first day of the week in memory of the day on which Christ rose;

—Sunday: means "belonging to the Lord."

Practice

—It is not the weekend that lends importance to Sunday, but the assembling together of the faithful.

—So that all without exception may respond to the call to assemble, the day, hour, and place of the assembly must be known by those concerned.

—Christians also gather together in various other groups (for prayer, reflection, concerted action) according to certain affinities (shared interest or preference, age, common cultural interest, etc.). The Sunday assembly differs from these in that faith is the sole criterion for attendance.

—This "public" assembly on Sunday offers a more complete sign of the church than these other gatherings. But it must not be broken up too much (too many Masses) or allowed to become insignificant.

—The Sunday assembly—different from the great feast-day assemblies—should remain human in its dimensions: talking to one another and other evidences of love should find a place here.

To receive the gift of God together

Significance

—The faithful do not assemble to be among friends but to:

—Hear God's word.

—To be of help to one another in any way possible and to act in solidarity with the world.

—To pray and give thanks.

—To share the eucharistic bread.

Practice

—The task of the assembly does not end with the celebration of the rites appropriate to it. God's word must enlighten and convert; what the faithful receive they must share; the church must shine forth to others through its members.

By celebrating the mysteries of the Risen Christ

Significance

—The assembly is not a public reception, nor a bible study group, nor a work of charity, nor an action group. . . .

—It is a "celebration": a meeting begotten of faith in the Lord who came to save the world.

Practice

—Nothing that we do (welcoming, speaking, singing, eating, etc.) can be reduced down to what meets our immediate understanding, feeling, and evaluating of each experience. It is more than this.

—From the opening moments of the assembly, the name of him who has gathered us together is invoked and reinvoked:

"The Lord be with you."

"And also with you."

—Everything happens in ways that are symbolic of our faith: we speak, God speaks; we give, God gives; we pardon, God pardons; we eat and God nourishes us.

Through different rites and symbols

Significance

—Every meeting of God and his people is done through symbolic actions.

—These are collective actions, patterned on familiar models so that the group can perform and understand them.

—The Mass unfolds based on several significant moments: the opening rite, the liturgy of the word, the Lord's Supper.

Practice

—To open the assembly, the pattern is the following:

we are assembled in the name of the Lord (first greeting).

we pray to him (prayer and *Amen*).

—This basic pattern is often enriched by other elements:

the gathering song.

a period of silence to allow the assembly to internalize what is happening.

a period in which to become reconciled with oneself, with our neighbors and with God.

a hymn of praise (*Gloria*).

—The gathering hymn is a festive community gesture in which the assembly

is knit together, takes shape, begins to celebrate by what it does.

positions itself before God by what it says.

In suitable groupings

Significance

—Although Christians can meet anywhere, they are helped in their celebration if they have a special place—their home—a church.

—The church should be practically arranged for celebration, but it should also show that it is a symbol of those assembled and of their faith.

Practice

—Each action calls for appropriate grouping
for hearing the word of God and sharing it,
for singing and praying together,
for setting the table and sharing in the meal.

—We must make the best possible use of existing places for celebration, considering the number of participants and the style of celebration, and not allow ourselves to be brought to a standstill because of unplanned or careless grouping.

—And what of latecomers? When the style of celebration adopted convinces participants that their celebrations exist only because of them and through their efforts (and not solely because of several persons "delegated to perform the rites") then the opening rites will no longer take place before empty seats....

2

PROCLAIMING THE WORD

How will they believe if the WORD is not proclaimed?

Faith is a response to the proclamation of good news: the gospel of the Risen Christ. When Christians assemble it is always for the purpose of:

—*Listening* to the gospel message

—*Responding to it* through prayer

In the assembly there is a word "exchanged," "given," "sealed": this is the covenant between God and his people.

Is every Christian celebration a Liturgy of the Word?

It is like a dialogue between God and his people, which hinges on the following words:

"All of you, listen to this!"

1. The PROCLAMATION of God's plan of salvation and the conditions for following Christ

—by Bible readings taken from the history of the people of God, before, during, and after the coming of Jesus.

—by all forms of PREACHING: homilies, explanations, exhortations.

—by the songs and prayers that repeat God's message to us today.

—by the images and symbols that allow something mysterious to be seen.

"Amen! We will adhere to all that God has said."

2. The ADHERENCE in faith of the assembled people to the message proclaimed

—by silence during which the word resonates within us and questions us.

—by the acclamations connected to the readings, the refrains of psalms and canticles, the verses of hymns.

—by the prayers that "confess" (= proclaim) the faith of the church.

"And now, Lord, do what...."

3. A PLEA for an answer
   —to the petitions expressed in the general intercessions.

—to the wishes expressed in song and prayer.

4. Here, when appropriate, occurs the sacramental pact (for example, the eucharist), the sign by which God and humanity commit themselves to one another, where the word "takes on bodily form."

God's word spoken by people

God speaks only when persons speak to other persons.

—Already in the Bible: the words of the prophets, of Jesus, of the Apostles, and of many others revealing the meaning of the history of the people of God.

—Now in Church assemblies there are:

lectors who read the Bible in the presence of the people;

prophets who show how timely the reading is for us today;

those who explain so that all may understand;

those who exhort and encourage;

those who pray before their brothers and sisters.

—God's word always comes to us through the words of believers:

when a priest presides, he has a particular responsibility (homily, presiding prayers) but his voice should not be the only one;

other voices can strengthen the faith of the participants, witnesses in the Spirit of what they believe and live;

the voice of the assembly that sings and prays is the active presence of the Lord.

How can I answer AMEN if I do not understand?

Everyone who addresses the assembly must be heard and understood:

—Scripture readings, prayer intentions, instructions, explanations;

—Bible verses or verses of songs sung by soloists or choral groups.

We must check on:

—the placement of the person speaking; can he/she be seen and heard?;

—the advisability of a sound system (necessary? properly used?);

—tone of voice and public speaking ability (see below);

—language and style (understood by everyone?);

—the musical accompaniment, and see to it that it does not drown out the singing.

The art of public speaking

It was said of Jesus: "No one has ever spoken as this man does."

1. Authority:

—The persons who transmit the word of God do not do it of themselves but with all the authority that comes to them from inspired scripture.

—The persons who witness, explain, exhort, do so with the assurance given them by the Holy Spirit.

2. Content:

—The reader of the Bible does not change a word of the text; the meaning of what is read is not limited to what the reader understands of it.

—In the spoken word, the faith of the church is always at issue.

3. Form:

—pronunciation (vigor of consonants; exactness of vowels);

—punctuation (appropriate pauses that make for understanding);

—good, true tone of voice;

—a clear, well-defined, well-balanced style.

What transcends the words

The word of God cannot be reduced to the spoken word.

—It is a person: Christ acting through the Spirit.

—The Spirit bears the LIVING WORD into the assembly not only through words and through what reason understands but also:

through bodily attitudes of adoration, supplication, praise;

through symbolic rites and gestures (word-in-act);

through poetry (in which not everything is expressed, leaving each one to search for new meanings);

through music which says more than the spoken word;

even through unfamiliar languages;

through everything presented for us to see;

through silence, sign of the Eternal Word.

3

RESPONDING TO THE WORD

"We will observe all that the Lord has decreed"

Exodus 24, 3

This was the unanimous response of the People of God to Moses when he returned from Sinai and "told them all the Lord's words and laws."

The appropriate way to respond to God's word is to put it into practice.

Matt. 7, 21 with the parable that follows

Jesus' teaching is clear and insistent: "It is not those who say to me, 'Lord, Lord,' who will enter the kingdom of heaven, but the person who does the will of my Father in heaven." And after the parable of the sower and the seed: "My mother and my brothers are those who hear the word of God and put it into practice."

Luke 8, 21

Word received, word given, fidelity to the word

But there is an intermediate step between the revelation of what God wills and its practical application by the faithful: an exchange of the word in a symbolic gesture. It is the pact of the Covenant. Just as marriage is the link between the love a man and woman offer each other and their life together, so celebration in liturgy and sacrament bridges the distance between the knowledge of God's design (evangelization) and living out what it implies (life in Christ). Liturgy is the act in which the word is exchanged. Here faith is received and given. It is the point of no return: it is the moment in which the fallible faith-fidelity of humanity is linked to the unfailing fidelity of God in the Risen Christ. The word has become sacrament.

Faith confessed

Usually, hearing the word is not sufficient preparation for really putting it into practice. To become the word of the Covenant, it must be professed before the believing community assembled to receive the word even as they celebrate it.

All liturgy is a "confession" of faith, that is, a public proclamation by the assembled church of its faith-filled allegiance to God's plan for salvation.

All liturgy is a proclamation of God's "marvels." But this proclamation is also "celebrated." It is celebrated in such a way that it becomes simultaneously a profession of faith and a committed response mediated by the action of the Holy Spirit.

Amen

Ps. 105, 48
Apoc. 5, 14; 19, 4

Amen is the basic form of the faith-filled response of the people to the word. The church's *Amens* resound from the liturgies of the Old Testament to the celestial liturgies of the Apocalypse: after each petition or prayer of thanksgiving, after doxologies and hymns and especially at the end of the eucharistic prayer—the church's confession of faith par excellence—in which the people's *Amen* ratifies the New Covenant in the blood of Christ.

Amen (taken from roots of Hebrew words meaning the truth and fidelity of God) signifies that which endures and will endure, something solid, something that relies on a faithful God. We give it our full assent; we commit ourselves in Christ Jesus to conform our conduct to it; and we pray that the reality may conform to our desires. "Thus it is and thus may it be." Here the past, present, and future of the Covenant converge.

Dialogue, songs, prayers

The celebration is surrounded, punctuated, held in momentum from beginning to end by dialogue and acclamations that make the people's "confession" a reality. From the opening greeting to the final sending forth, moving through the acclamations that surround the gospel (which is not simply an announcement), the dialogue at the preface, etc., the assembly's commitment to the word being celebrated can be judged by the response level at these moments of dialogue.

Songs function to spread out, make clear, prolong, and deepen all the varieties of responses: admiration, allegiance, meditation, petition, etc.

Prayers—active words—commit the assembly and the whole church to the work of the word, to laboring with it as it turns over the waiting soil, working, irrigating, enlightening, warming it, and furthering its growth.

Homily and sharing

In these moments the word is refracted through the believers who bear witness to the word. Hearts in which the seed has not yet taken root or which have been poorly watered are inspired to make a more generous and enlightened response.

Let us be good pedagogues and begin with essentials. Saint Ambrose said that, at Milan, the *Amens* of the assembly resounded like the awesome roar of the sea! What are the *Amens* of my assembly like and what do they signify as the people receive and celebrate their liberation in Jesus Christ?

4

PRAYING PETITIONING INTERCEDING

"What you have said, now do it"

Christians are people who gather together to hear the good news of their liberation in the Risen Christ; together they adhere to it in faith, singing, confessing, and celebrating their hope.

But the story does not stop there. Certainly the Risen Christ will die no more; he has won a definitive victory over death. Thus he is present and active in the middle of his people, and his kingdom is already here but not yet in its entirety. Death and sin continue their destruction. Trials strike his disciples. And many people have not yet received the Good News.

That is why the faithful assembled are not satisfied just to listen to the promise, to meditate on it, and to be thankful to God for it. They further add: "Lord, what you have said, now do it."

After readings and songs, prayers

Christian celebration symbolically summarizes the entire history of humanity's salvation: its past (recalling what God said and did that serves as the basis of our hope); its present (our conversion to the word and our sanctification through the eucharist); its future (expectation of the drawing together of all things in the risen Jesus).

This life cycle is expressed and lived out in the elements essential to the "liturgy of the word": biblical readings that recall past deeds; songs that are the faith response of the people present; prayers that are an appeal for their complete fulfillment in faith.

Unquestionably, prayer permeates the liturgy. But it has, in addition, its own special moments and characteristic forms. After the word has been heard, meditated on, responded to, and proclaimed, there comes the appropriate moment for supplication and petition. At Mass, the general intercessions conclude the liturgy of the word.

"Ask for the needs of all people"

Luke 18, 1
Luke 11, 9
Echoing the teaching of Jesus: "Pray without ceasing" and "Ask, seek, knock," the Epistle to Timothy offers Christian assemblies a basic principle for intercessory prayer:

"My advice is that, first of all, there should be prayers offered for everyone—petitions, intercessions and thanksgiving—and especially for kings and others in authority, so that we may be able to live religious and reverent lives in peace and quiet...for *1 Tim. 2, 1-2* God wants everyone to be saved...."

This text reminds us of three things:

1. The believer has to ask. The free gift of God comes to those who ask for it.

2. The Christian always asks in a "spirit of thanksgiving." Prayer must be offered confidently with the

certain conviction that God has already heard it.

3. The prayer of the assembled church is offered for all people because God wishes everyone to be saved.

A universal prayer

In restoring the common prayer of the faithful to the Mass, Vatican II's reforms gave the prayer the significant name of "universal prayer." *Four* directions for this prayer are mentioned:

—the church throughout the world;

—those in positions of responsibility in society;

—the most unfortunate among us;

—the assembled community.

What is the usual practice in our churches? Very often the prayers are responses to the word that has been heard or to current world events. That is alright in itself. But is it really a universal prayer? Are people prayed for? All categories of people? Perhaps people's horizons are too limited.

To bring clarity to a certain confusion in practice we should distinguish *three* things:

1. Witness-type intentions or reflections that are reactions of the faithful to the word proclaimed or to current events: this is a good way to share the word. It is connected with the homily. It is rarely a "universal" prayer. However, it should not disappear from the celebration for that reason.

2. Intentions for the universal prayer: it is the place to pray for *people* (not for ideas). The whole world is present at this moment. These intentions are *common* in the sense that each person present

should make them his or her own (if not, they are merely private intentions).

3. *Intentions-at-large* in their proper place after the common intentions: they can be personal ones because they are the responsibility of those who offer them to the charity of their brothers and sisters. But these latter are not obliged to make a public response to them.

A question of form

Each intention is offered by a voice (which can vary). The assembly makes the intention its own either by a silent prayer or by an answering refrain.

Helpful hints:

1. The best intentions are those that are simple and clear. The expression of too many thoughts, and wordiness, should be avoided. If not, by the end of the prayer we no longer know for whom or for what we are praying.

2. The simplest form is "Let us pray for..." followed by the names of people or the mention of a category of people. This form is recommended. The form "Let us pray for...(designated person) so that (favor requested)" is more complete. But in elaborating on the favor requested, the faithful should avoid detailing at length what God and their hearers are to think or to do....

Interceding

Interceding is to "take a step," to pledge one's word, to commit oneself to the request made. Each one has to do this interiorly in solidarity with those whose names are mentioned. Let each one judge his or her involvement.

If this were better understood, we would perhaps hear fewer protests about the straightforward type of phrasing such as "That the hungry be fed." The objection is made: "That is relying too easily and too much on God!"

Prayer intentions cannot be proposed to the assembly unless its members ask themselves:

—Do I believe that God wants what I am asking even more than I do?

—Do I exist in solidarity with the salvation history of humanity in Christ Jesus?

5

THE LORD'S SUPPER

BEGINNING THE EUCHARIST

1 Cor. 11, 20

The high point of the Mass consists in a prayer of thanksgiving. This prayer is part of a series of symbolic gestures which from the beginning of Christianity have been called "the Lord's Supper."

To this meal celebrated in memory of Jesus dead and risen, Christians soon added readings, songs, and prayers. So the whole Mass since the second century has consisted of two parts:

—the liturgy of the word (up through the general intercessions);

—the liturgy of the eucharist (from the carrying up of the bread and wine to the prayer after communion).

In this chapter we begin the study of the liturgy of the eucharist during which the Lord's Supper is celebrated.

Four original gestures

During this final meal with his disciples before his death and resurrection, Jesus wished to give a special meaning to several of his gestures. This is what is meant by his words: "You will do this in memory of me."

1 Cor. 11, 23–26

Thus was constituted a "tradition" related to us by St. Paul as well as by the Gospels of Matthew, Mark, and Luke. When their witness is compared, Jesus'

significant gestures can be reduced to four: con-
stituting the "this" that the church understood it was
to do in memory of him:

1. He *took* some bread and wine.

2. He *gave thanks* to God his Father.

3. He *shared* the bread.

4. He *gave* the bread *to be eaten* and the cup *to be
drunk*.

Program for the celebration

These four gestures constitute the structure of all
Christian eucharists. They form the plan for the
second part of the Mass:

1. Preparation of the gifts (bread and wine)

2. Eucharistic prayer

3. Breaking of the bread

4. Communion

Two types of actions are involved:

—the first set includes the *gestures* required by any
meal: to get the table ready and bring in the food, to
share this with the guests, to eat it. These actions
supply the framework for the rite of "The Lord's
Supper."

—Some *words* break through into the action. These tell
us that the meal is a festive meal, a religious act, the
memorial of Jesus saving humankind. A special
moment celebrates this: the great prayer of
thanksgiving.

It remains for us to see how the celebration expresses
these four movements of celebration.

The liturgy of the word ends after the general intercessions. What happens then?

—Current custom: People sit down. The collection is taken up. The organ plays. Or the priest says the words: "Blessed are you...." The paten and chalice are placed on the altar.

The words "The Lord be with you" mark the beginning of the eucharistic prayer rather clearly. But how can we tell we are beginning a meal? The Lord's Supper?

—A comparison might help: In the Byzantine liturgy, the eucharist begins with a "great entrance." The priest makes his way through the assembly carrying the bread and wine covered by a cloth. The "keroubikon," a solemn hymn, is sung simultaneously; the faithful bow or prostrate themselves. The Lord is entering for his Passover meal.

The rites for the Mass since Vatican II have also provided ways in which to accentuate the beginning of the Lord's Supper.

1. Preparation of the Table

Up until this point in the celebration, the altar ought not to have been the center of attention; it has not been used; it has been bare. The heart of the action has been in the assembly: words, songs, prayers.

Now the assembly gets ready for the meal:

—the tablecloth is put on (the table could even be brought in);

—candles and flowers are brought in;

—in some places participants gather around the altar.

2. The Offertory Procession

GIRM, 49

Having the faithful offer the bread and wine is a practice recommended by the *General Instruction of the Roman Missal.*

Is the assembly aware of the importance of this act? The eucharist is a mystery of sharing. To give us his life, Jesus first takes our bread, "which earth has given and human hands have made."

The celebration manifests this mystery of sharing by a twofold movement:

from the assembly to the altar with the offerings;

from the altar to the assembly, by sharing and communion.

It is a good idea for the faithful who carry the bread and wine to come from the back and pass through the assembly. Other offerings, including the collection, can be included in this act (but they are left in front of the altar).

3. Singing and Music

Provision is made for some singing at this point in the Mass. What should it be like? The purpose of the old "offertory hymn" of the Roman Mass was not to begin the eucharist, but to accompany the offering (collection or "offering") of the faithful.

The years 1930–1950 saw the writing of many "offertory hymns." They have had to be discarded because of the ambiguity of their purpose and content.

Just as the Mass begins with a song and the liturgy of the word with an acclamation, so singing and music constitute one of the best ways to begin the eucharist, which is an act of praise. The Roman Missal offers no sample texts as precedents. Here are some suggestions already used successfully.

—Something of the "hymn of mysteries" type giving a first expression of the mystery of sharing. For example: "Holy is God" (Isele) for cantor and assembly;

—Something of the "praise" type which already introduces the act of thanksgiving into the assembly. It is into this act together with the preface that the eucharistic prayer will be integrated. For example, Psalm 99 "Praise the Lord"—for the whole assembly; or a hymn like "Praise God From Whom All Blessings Flow."

—Some type of music played during the actions performed at this part of the Mass: instrumental or a selection accompanied by humming during which the assembly takes up an appropriate ferial or seasonal song.

Let us remember that the prayers of the priest are planned as private prayers. They "can" be said aloud. But it is better to wait until the preface to hear the voice of the presiding priest.

N.B.–and the collection?

In a growing number of assemblies—which find it satisfactory—the collection occupies its own place between the liturgies of the word and the eucharist. It is a quiet moment, a sort of intermission that allows the assembly to begin its act of thanksgiving with freedom of spirit and freshness of heart.

II: GIVING THANKS

The accounts of the Last Supper tell us that Jesus, taking bread and the chalice, "blessed them" and "gave thanks." What Jesus said in these prayers of blessing and thanksgiving is not recorded. More important than the words spoken, a *gesture* of praise has been passed down to us. This gesture of the Lord's Supper is also part of the "this" we are to do "in memory of him." It is "the eucharistic prayer."

A. The meaning of the gesture

The word "thanksgiving" makes us think of a "thank you," of "gratitude"; but this is only one of the aspects of the eucharistic gesture, which, considered in its totality, has a much richer and more comprehensive meaning.

"Let us lift up our hearts"

The dialogue that precedes the preface and opens the eucharistic prayer instills the basic attitude, the primary meaning of the gesture: to lift up, to bear on high. The Greeks called it "anaphora," the act of bearing something on high. It is what we call eucharistic prayer, for at this moment everything ascends upward.

Hands are raised up. The Hebrew root for the word that designates the sacrifice of "thanksgiving" (todah) is doubtless the root of the word hand(iad): the person who recognizes that God has saved him from death comes into the assembly and raises his hand to testify before all to the grace he has received and for which he is coming to "give thanks." This is the priest's gesture at the preface.

Voices are raised. We will come back to this.

Minds are raised up. In "lift up your hearts" the word heart, in its biblical sense, designates the mind, thought, memory, intelligence that must all be "turned toward God." This enables us to pass, through faith, from the visible to the invisible.

The Bread and Wine. Formerly the climax of the Roman Mass was the "great elevation." The gesture remains at the "through him, with him, in him." It is always moving in the same direction.

"We proclaim your resurrection"

St. Paul gives the principal meaning of the eucharistic prayer when he writes: "Whenever you eat this bread and drink this cup you proclaim the death of the Lord until he comes."

1 Cor. 11,26

The Title "Lord," as used here, refers to the Risen Lord.

So the eucharistic prayer is first a proclamation, an announcement, a recollection (a "memory," an "anamnesis") of the marvels God has worked among humankind—in creation, in salvation history, but particularly in Jesus, born of Mary, dead and risen, living and acting among his own until his second coming.

"We sing the hymn of your glory"

This is a public proclamation. It is a "confession." It spontaneously assumes the form of an act of praise and the form of a song.

The entire assembly of believers brings about eucharist. "We give thanks, we proclaim, we recall," etc.

—this remains true even if at certain moments a single voice speaks in the name of all.

—and united with the people assembled to give thanks, is the whole church in heaven and on earth, all visible and invisible creation.

The assembly gives thanks with all its strength and in a loud voice.

Thanksgiving (todah) in the psalms always takes the form of acclamation and singing, accompanied by music and instruments. The eucharist is seen in its wholeness as a song of praise.

"We offer"

In remembering the saving gestures of God, we offer him the "sacrifice" of thanksgiving, meaning ourselves, in Jesus, who offered himself once and for all to his Father. "It is love I desire and not sacrifice." Animal sacrifice is replaced by the "sacrifice of the lips," the prayer of praise. We do this over the shared bread and the blessing cup. But these are "presented" rather than "sacrificed." They are "sacrament" signs and symbols. The real sacrifice is the sacrifice of the heart that offers itself to the Father; because this is always done as an assembly, it is the spiritual sacrifice of the church. But the singing itself is also a sign and symbol of the eucharistic sacrifice. The persons who sing go forth using their breath and voice, and moving purposefully toward him whom they admire, praise, and love. They move toward the Father. And they do not go alone, but in the company of the assembly that praises "with a single voice."

B. Making eucharist

The reforms of Vatican II reestablished the eucharistic prayer as a proclamation made aloud and intelligible to the assembly. It has reassumed its authentic purpose as the most important profession of faith in the church. But by an act of reverse assertion, the content of the proclamation has relegated the form to the background: the form that should express the act of praise of the whole assembly.

In the "sung Mass" before the Council, singing accompanied everything (dialogue, preface, sanctus, benedictus, per omnia) and along with it church bells and hand bells. Now the eucharistic prayer often seems to be a long monologue recited by the priest, unbroken except for the "Holy holy, holy" and the acclamation of the anamnesis. This is truly deplorable.

"We and all your people"

In several places the Roman Canon expresses the fact that the people praise, recall, offer, pray. The new prayers always use "we." The true role of the priest who presides is only understood in connection with the whole assembly making eucharist together.

In the Copt liturgy, the prayer unfolds as an almost continuous dialogue among the priest, the deacon, the choir, and the people. In the institution narrative alone there are 17 moments of participation by the assembly.

Each culture has to find appropriate ways to signify the assembly's act of praise.

"Two steps, three movements"

If we do not know what Jesus said at the Last Supper, we do know something of the prayers of thanksgiving in use at his time.

First of all, biblical prayer has two steps:

1. "God, you who. . ." (proclamation of the marvels done, "anamnesis").
2. "Now do what. . ." (petition, "epiclesis")

Praise and petition are never separated. God is reminded of what he has done and wishes to do, so that it may all be done now and brought to completion. We remember "today" what is to come in the future, by focusing on the past.

But the tradition of eucharistic prayers has developed in three movements:

1. Praise to God—unsolicited admiration. This corresponds (in a general way) to the preface. Singing predominates; the assembly has a large part to play.
2. Thanksgiving for all God has done in human history; it ends by recalling the death and resurrection of Christ. The "founding" narrative of the Last Supper is included.
3. A network of requests so that this memorial meal may, through the action of the Spirit, consecrate those who take part in it, sanctify the church, and save all, living and dead.

A single flow

From the initial dialogue, which sets the act of praise in motion, to the final *Amen*, which concludes it, there is an immense flow of words, songs, gestures, one overlapping the other. This unity of action has needed rethinking since Vatican II, especially the role of song and gesture. The eucharistic prayers for children's assemblies (especially I and II) offer suggestions for the people's participation in the act of praise. But we still have to achieve the proper balance of each element: the appropriate synchronization of the priest's voice with the voices of the assembly, the role of musical instruments, the gestures that emphasize the essential moments and give form to the action of the assembly.

6

THE SHARING OF THE BREAD

A gesture with a message

Why did the Emmaus disciples recognize the risen Jesus at the moment he shared the bread? Why did Saint Luke describe the eucharist by the gesture of the sharing of the bread, the "fraction," in preference to any other?

Acts 20, 7; 2, 42

There are several possible answers; because the sharing of the bread is a very rich symbol, easily understood. It evokes simultaneously:

—the sacred law of hospitality universally accepted throughout the human race;

—the unceasing reminders in the Law, the Prophets,and the New Testament: "Share your bread with the hungry"

—the miracles of Jesus multiplying the loaves to signify that messianic times had arrived, since the promise had been fulfilled: "The poor will eat and be filled."

—one of the gestures by which Jesus at the Last Supper instituted the eucharistic meal to be done in his memory; a gesture that he repeats after his resurrection;

—the sign of agape, of fraternal love in the Holy Spirit, among the assembled Christians.

An important rite

What is to be thought of Masses at which, in less than three seconds and with a barely discernible gesture, the priest breaks "his host" in two—a host that he will consume entirely—and then proceeds to distribute pre-consecrated fragments to the assembly, fragments sometimes taken from the tabernacle?

This case aside, there are many ways to accentuate this gesture and give it meaning:

—use food easily recognized as bread when you look at it, touch it, taste it (only baker's bread will do!).

—bread or rolls that you can really share with guests.

—by a sharing gesture by the priest but continued by the ministers who are going to distribute communion, etc.

Let us remember the mystery of exchange, of reciprocal gift, of covenant, celebrated in the Mass: bread and wine came from the assembly and were carried to the altar. After having been made eucharist in a prayer of thanksgiving, they return to the assembly as God's bread and wine.

Another way to heighten its significance: those who brought up the offerings remain around the altar. They leave at communion time to distribute the eucharist. In their distribution they can break small pieces off from the larger ones.

We read in the Fathers of the Church: just as the risen Christ could appear to many at one time, so the eucharistic bread can be shared among all.

With respect, reconciliation, and joy

The attitude of the communicants should show what St. Paul recalls forcefully to us: that each one, by eating and drinking should know how "to discern the Body of Christ."

1 Cor. 11, 19

Whether the faithful are grouped around the altar, or in a procession from which each one approaches the altar; or the ministers separate and go to different places in the great assembly, respect for the *Body* implies mutual respect for those who constitute this *Body*.

All liturgies seem to wish to emphasize a moment of reconciliation, pardon, and penance between the eucharistic prayer and the communion:

—by the "Our Father": pardon us as we pardon. . .;

—by the sign of peace;

—by various gestures and words: "Lord, I am not worthy, but say. . ."

Acts 2, 46

Paschal joy is a characteristic note of the meal of Christians. This joy is expressed and shared in song.

The songs at the moment of sharing

After the Our Father and the sign of peace, the rites of sharing, which will end with the prayer after communion, are begun. Here singing plays an important role.

The Missal provides for three songs: the song at the fraction (*Agnus Dei*); the song during the communion; the hymn after communion.

It is not always possible or appropriate to sing all three of these songs. A judgment on what significance they have for the occasion and whether or not to use them, has to be made for each assembly and celebration.

1. The song at the fraction

In the Roman liturgy this song is represented by the "Lamb of God." It is a litany that can be lengthened or shortened depending on the length of the rite. This type of singing is popular and lends itself easily to participation by assemblies.

We might also add that this time of waiting and recollection before communion is an especially appropriate moment to express in song the various aspects of the rich mystery of sharing and communion. Because of this it is interesting to use—as they do in the Milanese liturgy—a variety of texts.

2. Singing during communion

While all are taking part in the Lord's Supper, the song can signify simultaneously:

—the attitude of those who receive the bread as a help in their daily living;

—the joy of receiving the life of the risen Lord;

—the fraternal union of the participants in the Spirit;

—praise for the gift received.

However, we often feel torn between several activities: moving about, eating, singing. The whole assembly cannot give its full attention to the singing. That is why people often prefer silence, music, or a choral selection.

If a song is to be sung by the assembly during communion it should be a selection that does not require involved participation: a simple refrain;

quiet moments. The song should be the primary responsibility of a choral group, soloists, instruments.

Sometimes the song begun at the fraction can be continued up to the beginning of communion—and even be picked up afterwards as a conclusion (as a hymn after communion). Fewer songs are used this way and they have a special importance.

3. The hymn after communion

When all have communicated, there should be a time of complete silence (silence of word, gesture, movement, music). This silence can then give rise to singing from the assembly that is now truly united and full. Sometimes this is the very best time of the Mass for singing.

Versed hymns are particularly appropriate here.

The meanings of these songs are the same as for communion hymns. But their distance from the ritual action adds to their joyfulness and communal quality.

Once the Mass is ended there is no need, except in special cases, to add a "concluding song." Do not the words "Go in the peace of Christ!" say clearly that it is ended and that one can leave?

And the cup?

There is a certain violence done at each Mass in solemnly recalling the Lord's command: "All of you, take and drink of it" and then not following his command. How will we ever change this? In the Roman Church we have ten centuries of non-use to overcome—this is something for which our Orthodox and Protestant brothers and sisters reproach us. There is also a lack of desire on the part of most of the faithful who do not yet understand the value of this sacramental sign—and they will only discover its value by sharing in it. There is also a lack of interest on the part of pastors and ministers, even a lack of conviction. Couldn't we at least revive the practice on occasions where sharing in the cup is possible, and gradually recover its true meaning?

PART II

THE SONGS
OF THE MASS

7

THE ROLE OF SONGS

Is this song appropriate for...?

In the liturgy we do not sing just any song at any time. The series of readings, songs, and prayers that constitute the celebration follow a certain order and have a special meaning.

When someone in charge of liturgy has to choose a song or music for a service, it should be chosen not only because it is beautiful, well known or easy to learn, but first of all because it will adequately fulfill the function for which it is chosen: opening song, dialogue, meditation on the word, etc. The liturgy planner should therefore understand the function of songs and ask: "Is this song appropriate for this function?"

In the following chapters we will treat the various songs of the Mass one by one to ascertain their function and point out what forms correspond most fully to each function. But before undertaking this detailed study we should recall that the liturgical function of a song is a complex reality not to be underestimated or oversimplified.

There are three types of functions: general "human" functions; particular "ritual" functions; and functions "symbolic" of the Christian mystery.

1. A human act

Singing is a human activity that allows a person to become more human. Granted that the liturgy is celebrated for the glory of God. But the glory of God consists in the fact that the person exists and lives fully. It comes as no surprise that the reasons given for Christians singing from the beginning of the church up to Vatican II are primarily human ones.

a) Singing gives added flavor and meaning to the *words* that are said and heard. It lends to the spoken word its full strength of expression and communication.

b) Singing *unites* those who sing. Use of the same tone and rhythm produces not only unison or harmony but a community.

c) Singing is celebration. It takes us beyond ordinary duties and practical tasks, opening out onto other aspects of existence: gratuitousness, freedom, love.

2. A ritual action

A rite is primarily a predetermined activity that must be carried out. If music enters into its progression, it does not do so as an end in itself, as is the case when "one makes music." It is only one of many elements integrated into a whole, as we see in opera, film, shows. (A) Most frequently it is linked to the spoken word, sometimes to an action without words. (B) It is performed by a variety of participants: an individual, a whole group, part of a group. All of these things are components of the ritual function of music.

A. Music must be adapted to the type of WORD proclaimed or the action performed. It can be highlighted or serve as background.

a) To *proclaim* a biblical text, a preface, a prayer intention: there is a message to be transmitted. The word should be clear and understandable. Music is needed only to sustain the tone of voice and accentuate the rhythm of the words. It is not really a song but a recitative, a chant.

b) To *meditate on* a psalm, the Our Father, a prayer: there is a word to be absorbed, to be tasted, to be assimilated. Even if I say it with others, I am not proclaiming it to others; I am saying it to myself. I am not yet singing it. I am interiorizing it and becoming identified with it. It remains a recitative, but a recitative turned inward.

c) To *sing one's prayer,* anthem, tropary or psalm refrain: the word is diffused melodically and rhythmically. It becomes a song. The music permeates me but without ever totally submerging the word, as, for example, in the Gregorian anthems or eastern troparies. This is called verbal-melodism.

d) To *sing* a hymn, choral number, song, *together:* because of the poetry, poetic line and meter, there is a pre-determined rhythm that the music uses and reinforces; because of the regular stanzas, an independent, well-balanced melody results. The text forms the basis of the singing. But the music has the leading role. This is the ideal form for group singing.

e) To *acclaim* the *Amen, Alleluia,* Glory to you, O Lord: the words and syllables are used primarily to give support to a "cry," to a collective reaction to an event. It is a strong action, with minimal verbal emphasis, more or less rich musically.

f) If there is no spoken word: There can be

vocalization or instrumental music during a period of meditation or during a procession (offertory, communion), always adapted, of course, to the spirit of the moment.

The following table sums up this text-music relationship:

WORD ⟵--	
---⟶	MUSIC
Spoken	Vocalization
Language	Instruments
PROCLAMATION	ACCLAMATION
"Chanting"	
MEDITATION	HYMN
Psalmody	Choral
SINGING	
"Verbal-melodism"	

B. In considering the function of singing we should also consider *the music,* the persons who sing or play:

a) Sometimes it is an individual:

—the presiding priest (prayers, prefaces, dialogues);

—a psalmist at the lectern (psalm verses);

—a cantor, an animator (verses of hymns, prayer intentions);

—a solo voice in the choir;

—an instrumental solo.

b) At times the whole assembly:

—responses to the celebrant, acclamations, refrains, hymns.

c) At times, a group:

—a part of the assembly (children, men, women);

—a choral group (for versicles, couplets, motets);

—instrumentalists

According to the choices made above, there will be dialogued, alternating, or sustained forms, repetition, and concatenation, etc.

3. A symbolic gesture

The function of singing is not limited to materially accomplishing the rite. Its purpose, thanks to a rite accomplished in faith and through the Holy Spirit, is to open minds and hearts to the mysteries celebrated: to accept the word and respond to it (not only with lips), to meditate and acclaim, to petition and give thanks, to adore and to love.

Here it is impossible to detail all that singing effects. Everything depends on the individual response to the symbolic content of the rite: each one has to find the meaning appropriate for him or her and commit to it freely from the depths of his or her being.

However, the "atmosphere" in which the celebration is carried out is of capital importance in helping or hindering these deep responses, depending on people's perception of it as beautiful or ugly, a help to recollection or distracting, dynamic or boring, joyous or sad, individualistic or unifying, etc.

8

DIALOGUES AND ACCLAMATIONS

The cry of the saved

What can be more upsetting than the measured cry of a crowd crying for bread or freedom? What more creative of enthusiasm than cries of victory, festive shouts?

The people of God cry out, too, to the Only One who can save them from death: Help! Save us! Deliver us! Have pity on us! *Kyrie eleison!*

The company of the elect cries out, too, with joy celebrating its resurrection in Christ: *Alleluia! Hosanna! Gloria!* Long live God! *Amen!*

The psalms, prayer of the people of God, are full of these cries, appeals or joyous shouts. They are also woven into the Christian liturgy. But too often they cannot be properly appreciated because of the banality of the words used, the mournful tone and falling action of the melody "...through Christ Our Lord. *Amen*,"—"the Gospel of Jesus Christ..."— "Glory to you, Lord." This all bears little resemblance to the cries described above or to an acclamation, their stylized form.

At Mass

Nevertheless the *General Instruction of the Roman*

Missal strongly insists on this element of celebration:

14. *Since by nature the celebration of Mass has the character of being the act of a community, both the dialogues between celebrant and congregation and the acclamations take on special value; they are not simply outward signs of the community's celebration, but the means of greater communion between priest and people.*

15. *The acclamations and the responses to the priest's greeting and prayers create a degree of the active participation that the gathered faithful must contribute in every form of the Mass, in order to express clearly and to further the entire community's involvement.*

Between the initial greeting "The grace and peace of God our Father..."—"Blessed be God..." and the sending forth "Go in peace"..."Thanks be to God," the ritual of the Mass comprises no less than seventeen dialogued interventions that lead up to an acclamation by the entire assembly—and this does not include the penitential preparation and the general intercessions when they take on the form of a litany with a supplicatory refrain.

The important moments are the opening of the celebration, the amens that conclude prayers, before and after the Gospel, the dialogue before the Preface and the Sanctus, the acclamation for the anamnesis and the conclusion of the eucharistic prayer "through him...—*Amen!*" and that of the Our Father "For the kingdom...," the sign of peace, the final blessing and the sending forth.

Do we really know what we are depriving ourselves

of by not making these moments times of real acclamation?

1. A united group

When unified individuals are capable of acclaiming together, when they can "cry" out on the same tone and with the same rhythm their deep desires, their faith, their expectations, they strongly reinforce their cohesiveness, and at the same time send out a telling message of their unanimity. In the case of Christians, these are the ones who make the church and show that they do.

2. Spirited action

The liturgy is an action. But sometimes there is so much of the spoken word that the collective action gets lost. Ritual dialogues and acclamations are primarily actions. The content of the words used (*Amen, Alleluia,* Have mercy...) are secondary. In the foreground is the event and the response to it: the *gesture* of praise or call for help.

Of all the forms of singing, acclamation and dialogue are the most provocative of action, but only if we allow them to be so!

3. Concerted action

We are not in a crowd shouting out cries or slogans. We are in an assembly that finds itself called in the name of the Lord by one or another of its members having the grace of this ministry; we are an assembly that answers, thereby taking a position expressive of its faith.

Except for some rare cases, the ritual acclamations make a response to a voice (priest, deacon, animator). They bring alive the "dialogue between God and his people."

4. The framework of the celebration

As a rite, the celebration rests on a certain number of things that have to be done: entering, greeting, singing, praying, etc. When you study the inventory of Mass songs, it strikes you that the dialogues and acclamations are divided up in such a way as to structure the action, to open and close important events such as the Gospel or eucharistic prayer.

We are talking of fixed, firm points that could serve as a basis for celebration. When ministers and assemblies are accustomed to these fixed points, they feel comfortable and secure. Even with rather unskilled ministers and groups of faithful, an adequate ritual "level" can be maintained.

5. Unchanging songs

Dialogues and acclamations form part of the singing tools needed to focus oneself in the celebration. Let us forget for a moment our concern with the varying ferial or feastday songs, those typical of certain regions or parishes. Let us admit that every Catholic can participate at least by answering loudly and wholeheartedly to the "*Amen*," "Glory to you, Lord," "Praise to you, Lord Jesus," "It is right and just," "We proclaim your death"...etc. This is no small thing! And it can be done, provided that the opportunity for acclaiming is made available!

6. Appropriate tones of voice

Anarchic cries or the scanning typical of demonstrations are not appropriate for the eucharistic liturgy.

So the rhythm and tone must be stylized but not to such a degree that the acclamation becomes the melody for a hymn. This is the reason for the traditional, studied, linear tone used currently in France. This is not done because other voice tones are lacking, but because it is the tone that best suits this special ritual moment.

Polyphonic acclamations can produce beautiful results, but in choosing this style we may have to forego the participation of a part of the assembly!

Images of a celestial liturgy

In the celestial liturgies John contemplated and described in the Apocalypse, each of the groups participates through acclamation: the four living creatures, the twenty-four ancients, the angels, creation, separately or together, as a "model" for our earthly liturgies.

Thus from the New Testament to the parousia, the words of the psalm are verified:

Psalm 89, 16

"Happy the people who learn to acclaim you!
Yahweh, they will live in the light of your favor;
They will rejoice in your name all day...."

9

THE OPENING RITE

This section deals with everything that takes place at the beginning of Mass: from the welcome given one another to the first reading. Here is a pertinent text from the *General Instruction of the Roman Missal:*

24. *The parts preceding the liturgy of the word, namely, the entrance song, greeting, penitential rite,* Kyrie, Gloria, *and opening prayer or collect, have the character of beginning, introduction, and preparation.*

The purpose of these rites for the assembled faithful is:

—To help them bring about communion.

—To dispose themselves to hear the word of God clearly and to celebrate the eucharist worthily.

This important text suggests the following thoughts:

1. Here we are concerned with only an "introduction," a preparation for what is to follow. We should not, therefore, turn this into a celebration nor devote a disproportionate part of the Mass to it. It is sufficient to arouse the assembly's desire for the word to come without absorbing too much of their attention and interest.

2. All five of the elements listed as opening rites are not of equal importance nor do they fulfill the same functions. The entrance song is not obligatory; the

Kyrie may be combined with the penitential preparation, which is sometimes better placed elsewhere than at the beginning (listening to the word is an especially appropriate moment for acknowledging our sinfulness). The *Gloria* is not always required or appropriate. We have to target what is essential.

3. The essence of the opening rite, which is (a) to act as church and (b) prepare ourselves, consists ritually in two actions:
—the greeting of the presiding priest who brings the assembly together "in the name of the Lord";
—the prayer by which all turn toward the Lord who is coming into our midst.

The remaining elements should be so organized as to constitute the best possible beginning for the whole celebration.

The opening song

After everyone has assembled and welcomes are over, a common symbol is needed to help the group enter into the celebration together. This could be a moment of silence, a poetic text, music, the bringing in of the Cross, the illuminating of an icon, etc.

However, of all possible symbolic actions—and several can be used simultaneously—singing is the most efficacious means of properly beginning the celebration. Let us quote again from the *General Instruction of the Roman Missal*:

25. *After the people have assembled, the entrance song begins, and the priest and ministers come in. The purpose of this song is to open the celebration,*

deepen the unity of the people, introduce them to the mystery of the season or feast, and accompany the procession.

This makes *four* functions for the opening song clear to us. Each one invites our reflection.

1. Opening the celebration

Singing is the first of the community's actions. It sets the assembly in motion.

What if people have not arrived yet? This is a place for some education. We cannot celebrate without one another.

What if we have just had a singing rehearsal? If so, haven't we cut the ground out from under our feet? And yet why couldn't this rehearsal (unless it is done for purely technical reasons) be part of the preparation signified by the opening rite? If several songs have to be prepared, keep the opening song for last and let the rehearsal flow smoothly into the real celebration.

2. Drawing the assembly together

One of the graces inherent in singing is that it can be an expression of personal and collective faith simultaneously. This is the source of its symbolic power to unite.

But to achieve this, everyone who wants to participate must be able to do so at least through the refrains or repetitions. A song that is too difficult or one that is too new is less effective than one that is well known and easily sung. We have to be aware of this, not be satisfied with the same old thing, but be able to plan wisely, deliberately, purposefully.

How many verses or couplets are needed for the

assembly to really begin singing and celebrating? Often more than a hurried presider is prepared to accept!

3. Preparing the mind

Every song has a text. This is more or less important depending on the circumstances, the music, the style. At the opening of the celebration the common act of singing often takes on more importance than the text itself. This is natural.

Liturgy animators, however, are right to concern themselves with seeing to it that the text of the song chosen directs minds toward the day's liturgy. Let us remember, though, that on an ordinary Sunday the assembly has not yet heard the day's readings. If we do not wish to over anticipate or weaken the assembly's receptivity, we have to simply pique the faithful's interest, awaken a desire to hear more. Requiring the opening song to always announce the theme of the day's readings is going too far!

If there is a good reason for drawing attention to the text of the opening song, it would be better placed after the greeting. The instruction could introduce it. It would then be sung "for itself."

4. Accompanying the entrance of the priest

This was formerly its principal function (introit) and the reason for its current name, "entrance song." This is now a secondary function. Whether or not there is a procession, whether or not the priest is present from the beginning or enters as the singing progresses, the basic importance of the role of the entrance song in connection with the whole assembly (including the priest and other ministers) remains.

10

SONGS COMPLEMENTARY FOR THE OPENING RITE

When we spoke of the Opening Rite of the Mass we recalled that it consists essentially in the gathering together of a believing people in the name of the Lord. Its structure is clear from a succession of three actions: the song, the greeting, the opening prayer. That is why we characterized as "complementary songs" the "Lord have mercy" and the *Gloria*.

In the old Latin sung Mass, the *Kyrie* and the *Gloria* were considered among the most important songs of the entire Mass. In reevaluating the opening song by adding the participation of the assembly, by creating a "penitential preparation" that includes the *Kyrie*, by recalling that the opening rites were only an "introduction and preparation" to the word and to the eucharistic meal, liturgical reform has changed our former practice.

KYRIE ELEISON

"Lord have mercy"

In the Roman Mass the singing of the *Kyrie* at the beginning of the rite doubtless marked the remains of a litany that had "arisen" in this place in the liturgy. There remained only the Greek invocation *Kyrie eleison, Christe eleison,* with no clear intention of stimulating prayer. With time, though, the invocations became so melodically developed that the *Kyrie* became an independent hymn.

The current missal provides two solutions for this confusion

1. The *Kyrie* is sung for itself after the penitential preparation. The people participate by repeating each invocation. Brief tropes may be inserted, meaning that each invocation may be prefaced by an intention. In this case the *Kyrie* is not penitential. It is a song in which the faithful acclaim the Lord and implore his mercy.

GIRM, 30

2. The "Lord have mercy" is integrated into the penitential preparation as a response to requests for pardon. In this case the *Kyrie* is not sung later.

The current practice

Since the liturgical reform, it has tended in the second direction. This practice can be continued while remembering certain things:

a) The literal translation: "Lord, have mercy—Christ, have mercy," does not offer much material for an acceptable song text. The words, not having any feminine syllables, are abrupt; the sounds are almost all muted and colorless; the rhythmic flow is too brief. So many people may prefer responses that further extend the song of the assembly, e.g., "Have pity on us, Lord" or "Pardon us and change our hearts."

b) If the form of the penitential preparation has not included the invocation "Lord, have mercy," or if for any reason, the call to penitence has been placed elsewhere in the Mass, it does not seem necessary to sing the *Kyrie* as a separate song.

c) It is desirable that we do not completely give up the use of the venerable ecumenical invocation: *"Kyrie eleison—Christe eleison."* From the beginning of the church these universally-known words have occupied their own particular place just as the *Amen* and *Alleluia* have.

d) An excellent opening for an ordinary Sunday or a weekday Mass is to begin with a great invocation of the *Kyrie* set either to a Gregorian melody or in a developed form such as we find in this text:

Holy God, holy strong God, holy immortal God,
KYRIE ELEISON

You who have suffered for us on the Cross,
CHRISTE ELEISON

Remember us when you enter into your Kingdom,
KYRIE ELEISON

e) Notice that in all these songs the word LORD (KYRIE) refers to Christ.

THE GLORIA

The "Glory to God in the highest" is a Christian hymn developed between the second and fourth centuries and used in the liturgy for the morning office. It was introduced into the Roman Mass for great feast days, then for all Sundays (except in Advent and Lent).

It is a model of Christian prayer in which praise and petition mingle together in a trinitarian progression. "...the Church assembled in the Spirit, praises and prays to the Father and the Lamb." It would be well

GIRM, 31

for all Christians to know this text by heart and be able to sing it together. We are lucky to have a French text that is beautiful, musical, rhythmic and easy to set to music.

Are there too many songs in the Opening Rite?

Isn't it too much to have an opening rite that comprises an entrance song, a *Kyrie* and a *Gloria*? If we really mean it should be a "preparation," why do we make it into an entire office, spending time that would be better used devoted to the word? These are valid objections. They often lead to the recitation of the *Gloria*. This practice is not meaningless, but soon becomes routine and tiring. Above all, it leads to abandoning the practice of singing the *Gloria*.

There are two possible solutions to this problem:

1. The singing of the *Gloria* can be used as an enrichment for feastdays, on Sundays in the Paschal season, and each time it has a significant contribution to make; but not routinely every Sunday.

2. It can sometimes be used—for example on Sundays after Christmas—as an Opening Song. This focuses new attention on it.

Music that is too complicated accompanying a text that is too long?

The *Gloria* is an ancient hymn in prose (not yet formed into verses and poetic lines). To sing it properly requires a sustained form of music that

changes from beginning to end. This is not a
popular style of music and requires training.
Parishes do not always have the free time to do this,
particularly if they do not have a choral group.

Two remarks can be made about this objection:

a) Parishes that have made the effort to learn one or
several melodies for the *Gloria* have not regretted
their decision. Just the opposite is true—they have
become quite attached to this practice—provided
always of course that the melody was well chosen
and that the music had enough staying power to ac-
commodate itself to continual use.

In these parishes the assembly often sings more than
elsewhere because there is a "fixed" song that
everyone knows by heart. And particularly because
it is a long song in which there is sufficient time to
make oneself comfortable in a truly musical moment
and in a collective choral action. This is unique in
our current Mass, which is often made up of odds
and ends of singing.

b) It is useful to have a more popular choral form
for this hymn, such as "Gloria of the Bells" by
C. Alexander Peloquin. It has met a very great need.
Still other texts can be written (e.g., Ps. 20 for
choir and assembly). But none of these can ever
completely replace the traditional text.

11

THE LITURGY OF THE WORD AND SINGING

Celebrating the word

The word of God can be approached in many ways: Bible study—individually or collectively, listening to sermons, homilies, lectures, courses; silent meditation, etc. All these complement one another: information, explanation, prayer.

But in the liturgy the word is first and foremost "celebrated." It is received by a group of people assembled in the faith of the church; a people that knows that God speaks to them and that they have an answer to give him. If further information and explanations are to be given, the entire experience is bound up in the liturgy—a collective symbolic and religious experience that nothing can replace.

If our Masses since Vatican II have been accused of being too loquacious, explanatory, didactic, is it not because we have forgotten that the liturgy of the word is not only making a statement in words and ideas, but that it is also a celebration?

Singing and the Word

Among the various elements that turn the word into a "celebration" (role of lectors and others with speaking parts, places and movements chosen, books, etc.), the most common element, which is also the richest, is singing—and music.

Singing and music allow the entire potential of the enunciated word to be operative (the word always implies more than it says and tries to put into practice what it says in words):

by dynamically proclaiming astonishingly good news;

by repeating it, meditating on it, savoring it, assimilating it;

by singing it, "professing" and "confessing" it, simultaneously;

by being jubilant because of the marvels and enchantment it finds.

Too many words and not enough singing

What have we accomplished of this fine, proposed program? Between the first reading, which opens the liturgy of the word of the Mass, and the general intercessions, which conclude it, what music do we find? Most often, and often the best performed: a psalm refrain, an *Alleluia*, another refrain at the general intercessions. We might call these mini-moments, lasting several seconds. Is this enough to create a celebration out of the mass of words used?

It is true that there is very little help on this subject in Paul VI's missal. In the ancient sung Mass there was only singing (even the readings!); now we have nothing sung but the responsorial psalm (if it is sung), the acclamation at the gospel (idem), the response at the intercessory prayers (idem), the *Credo* (idem), and improvised sequences for several feasts. So sometimes we have almost nothing. What is to be done?

Words immersed in song

The objective here is not to provide a great number of songs nor lengthy songs but to create a singing atmosphere that assures space and importance for the words. Here is a short, concrete program.

1. The opening acclamation for the procession of the Book.

Each important ritual act needs a sign, a key, an initiative symbolism: the opening hymn and the entrance of the Cross, to call the assembly together; the bringing of the bread and wine to the table, for the Lord's Supper. In certain Eastern rites the liturgy of the word opens with a "minor entrance": the deacon carries in the book crying: "O Wisdom!" There is nothing to prevent our doing the same: everyone having been seated after the collect (a note of introduction is often necessary before the readings), the lector passes through the assembly holding up the Lectionary while everyone sings "Glory to Christ, Eternal Word. . . ." If you try this you will find that when the reader begins to speak, his or her relationship with the assembly will be different and the word will be heard in a different way. However, the experience is better derived from practice than from explanation.

2. The psalm (see chapter 12)

3. Acclamations at the Gospel

The singing of the *Alleluia* (or its equivalent for Lent) can be thought of in two ways:

As a song pure and simple, playing the same role between the second reading and the gospel as the responsorial psalm does between readings one and two. In this case, if there is only one reading before the gospel, it can be omitted.

As an introduction to the gospel, which is then enclosed between a sung introduction and conclusion and assumes the special status of a celebrated statement. This is all done standing.

In practice, the *alleluia*—the opening dialogue—and the concluding acclamation, should be seen as a whole, as the framework, a "carrying case" for the gospel word. Obviously the desired effect will not be produced unless this is all done in song. To simply say these words has no meaning; it even becomes a sign that runs counter to what is intended.

4. Chanting the readings

We cannot deal with this subject here. But we are bringing it up because it is not a closed issue; this practice will return. Singing the gospel of the Nativity at Christmas or musically accompanying one of the prophecies is not farfetched. The practice of reading was adopted to make sure that information was passed on to the assembly—and this often remains the uppermost concern. But when this has been done, why can't the content of the information be celebrated?

5. The hymn after the Gospel

After the reforms of Vatican II it was talked about: after the readings (and homily) shouldn't we take the time to repeat, to savor, to sing of the word once again? Ritual history shows this need in the development of proses and sequences and in the Lutheran cantate. But not much progress has been made. Priority has been given to the spoken word (homily or sharing) and the *Credo*. The Mass is becoming too long. There is not enough time. But how do we want to make use of the time we have? Those who sing the hymn after the gospel, at least on certain days, know how worthwhile it is. Perhaps this could be considered the "grand finale" of the liturgy of the word. We will no doubt be speaking of this song and its role again.

6. The Credo (see chapter 13)

7. The General Intercessions

This is not properly meant to be a song. But a well chosen refrain sung by everyone really expresses the supplication of the assembled people.

May I remark in passing that we probably gave up too quickly on the set, chanted intentions (e.g., Byzantine Litany). With or without humming or organ, on certain days the sung litany constitutes a very celebratory and moving type of prayer.

8. To keep in mind

The lyrical homily (preaching varied with the insertion of refrains) has existed since Meliton of Sardes (second century) and is always interesting when done by those who know how to handle it.

Organ improvisation during the silence that follows the homily can be very enriching.

Copies of the verses of a song distributed during the liturgy of the word and linked to the readings is another way (in certain circumstances) of maintaining a songlike atmosphere.

After a liturgy of the word has been well celebrated and sung, we can progress smoothly to the "sacrifice of praise," the eucharistic meal.

12

THE PSALM

The liturgy of the word at Sunday Mass and on feast days is usually composed of four biblical texts:

Old Testament

Psalm

Epistle

Gospel

On opening the Lectionary or a missal of the faithful, you will notice that the second text listed above differs from all the others. Its form is that of a poem to be sung. A single book of the Bible is its source: the book of 150 psalms. But the reader will notice at the same time that the psalm unifies the other biblical readings. It does so in two ways:

1. In reading the psalm you see that it was chosen in harmony with the first reading we have just heard and also with the day's Gospel.

2. Because of the poetic language of the psalm, all that is said in the liturgy of the word is clothed in reality. For example, on the day of the Ascension: *Ps. 47* "God rises to shouts of acclamation."

When the church prays the psalms, it is not going back in time to the era before Christ. It understands all that is said in the light of Jesus, born a man, dead, risen, exalted. Everything God has done to save humankind is fully realized in him.

The three principal functions of the psalm at Mass

1. To announce the Word

What God is and what he has done for humankind is announced in the psalms as it is in the rest of the Bible. Here as in the other readings, God speaks to his people.

2. To respond to the Word

The psalm differs from the other biblical readings in that it is also a response to the word of God. The psalms are hymns and prayers of God's people which express their faith, praise and petitions. The psalm thus becomes the praise and prayer of the assembly.

3. To meditate on the Word

The assembled people, by making the psalm their own, by receiving into their mouths the inspired words, by letting them descend into their hearts, "eat," ponder, ruminate on the word so as to be better nourished by it. When received with faith, the word will burst forth not only in liturgical praise but in a whole life of charity.

Various forms

In the course of its long history the psalm has assumed various forms at Mass. Each one has had its own particular emphasis:

—The simple reading-announcement done by the lector.

—The responsorial song in which the whole assembly

associates itself to the psalmody and "responds" to the word by a short refrain.

—The gradual—a composition for a cantor and schola, which adds a rich melody to some few words, giving the assembly a period of meditation.

The reforms of Vatican II have retained a mixed form under the name of "responsorial psalm," which links up the functions of announcing and responding.

GIRM, 36

The psalmist or cantor of the psalm sings the verses of the psalm at the lectern or other suitable place. The people remain seated and listen, but also as a rule take part by singing the response....

GIRM, 36

There are a great number of ways to use the psalm at Mass including the assembly's saying of the psalm "straight through" and without a refrain. Practically speaking we can group these variations around three principal types.

A. The announced psalm

A reader does a poetic reading of the text—a reading that respects the blank spaces at the end of lines and leaves breathing space between the words. In this style the prayer of the psalms enters the mind of the listener through hearing. This style is very valuable and has helped many people "discover" the psalms.

Music can enter into the reading either as a musical background, as a melody for the psalmist, as harmony for a choir—if poetic listening is respected.

This does not exclude the assembly's participation by repeating several words or passages of the singing.

B. The psalm responded to

The whole assembly participates in the psalmody by repeating a refrain. It thus reacts to the statement made in the psalm. It begins to respond to the word. A dialogue is initiated between the psalmist and the assembly, image of the dialogue between God and his people.

Depending on the way the refrain is worked into the psalm, we have to make the following distinctions:

—the authentic form of the psalmody-responsorial: the refrain is fully integrated into the psalm; it is short and frequently repeated. It is a lively form inviting participation but which presupposes a very participatory assembly.

—the psalmody accompanied by a refrain: the refrain is a separate anthem inserted between the verses of the psalm. This is a practical solution for most assemblies. It is the one suggested in the Lectionary.

C. The recited psalm

The assembly's participation is no longer limited to a refrain. Everyone says the text straight through in unison or alternating verses. Each one can thus make his or her own the very words of the psalm either by collective recitation or by chanting on a simple psalm tone.

This form supposes that the members of the assembly have a copy of the psalm text, for example a song book with a good number of choices and the text arranged for psalmody. Many hymnals in the United States have made the psalms available to the assembly, and inexpensive editions of the entire

Psalter are appearing in the pew racks of U.S. parishes. Where used, participation is widespread. They awaken taste for psalm prayer. Remember that you are not limited to the single psalm indicated in the Lectionary: you may choose among some few others, provided that the psalm chosen can be adapted to the needs of the celebration.

13

"I BELIEVE IN GOD"

Before speaking of the *Credo* ("I believe in God")
of the Mass, which is a formula or symbol for professing one's faith, we must recall that the most
important profession of faith during the Mass is the
eucharistic prayer: it is addressed to the Father, proclaims the mysteries of Christ's life, and invokes the
Holy Spirit. It was the saying of the eucharistic
prayer in a low voice when it was no longer playing
its proper role that introduced the *Credo* into the
Mass.

The *Credo* does not belong to the basic structure of
the Mass. Depending on the liturgy, it is found just
before the eucharistic prayer, or before Communion, or after the gospel. It is in this latter place that
it was introduced among the Franks in the form of a
collective song. In France it became particularly
popular with the Masses of DuMont (17th century).

Place and meaning of the Credo

When Vatican II restored the intercessory prayers to
the Mass, this rite should normally have been linked
to the readings and the homily. After the announcement of the word come the requests. ("Do what
you said. . ."). But the *Credo* was too set in practice
as a follow-up to the gospel or sermon. It was left in
the place where it often regrettably interrupts the
progression of word, silence, prayer. We can't
blame those who have experienced the beautiful

reality of the traditional, logical progression described above for wanting to preserve it.

The instructions in the missal are limited to recalling the possible meanings of the *Credo*:

The symbol or profession of faith in the celebration of Mass serves as a way for the people to respond and to give their assent to the word of God heard in the readings and through the homily and for them to call to mind the truths of faith before they begin to celebrate the eucharist.

GIRM, 43

Three forms of profession of faith

There are many forms of profession of faith in the New Testament and in tradition. We have kept three principal ones.

1. The liturgical form in the baptismal symbol. It is the formula used for the baptismal ritual and the Easter vigil. It is written in the form of questions. But it can be considered as a basic collective confession.

2. The catechetical form for the introduction of catechumens. It is the recitation of the essentials of faith serving as a basis for Christian initiation and explanation of the faith. Our Apostles Creed corresponds to this form.

3. The theological or conciliar form detailing the dogma needed to answer the errors of heresy. The Nicene Creed, which became part of the Roman Mass between the ninth and eleventh centuries, corresponds to this form.

Pastoral and practical helps

Three solutions—and a fourth—have been found:

1. Sung in its entirety

Based on the Latin Mass, some of the first Masses following the Vatican Council suggested melodies for communal semi-recitative singing in the Gregorian style. These were little used. This long song unbalanced the overall time progression of an ordinary Mass. Besides, the creed is not a hymn. It is a text more appropriate for recitation than for singing. This is more evident in the vernacular than in Latin.

2. Common recitation

This is the most widely used practice. The results are often mediocre and boring. Diction more demanding than singing is needed to make it successful. Alternating sections between the celebrant and the assembly helps a little, but does not solve the problem. The creed is a celebratory low point in many Masses especially when placed between the homily and the general intercessions.

3. Insertion of a refrain

This is an easy, comfortable solution. Someone recites the text. The assembly inserts a refrain. In addition, I would like to suggest combining the refrain with a solo recitative accompanied or not by a choral group.

A further adaptation to the Nicene Creed and the Apostles Creed found in all missals and liturgical books, I would like to point out the use of the baptismal creed, combined with an optional sung refrain.

We believe in God the Father Almighty, creator of heaven and earth. (R)

We believe in Jesus Christ, His only Son, our Lord who was born of the Virgin Mary, suffered the passion, was buried, is risen from the dead and is seated at the right hand of the Father. (R)

We believe in the Holy Spirit, in the holy Catholic Church, in the communion of saints, forgiveness of sins, the resurrection of the body, and life everlasting. (R)

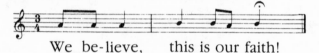

We be-lieve, this is our faith!

4. The song after the Gospel

The role of the *Credo* of the Roman Mass has been looked upon as a sung response to the Lord. The liturgy of the word certainly requires such a period of lyrical expression. However, I have certain questions: Why must it always be the same text? Why must all the mysteries of faith be detailed? Couldn't one particular thought from the readings be selected and pondered in depth? Couldn't it all be done in a really singable form?

14

EUCHARISTIC PRAYER AND SINGING

Center and summit

Now the center and summit of the entire celebration begins: the eucharistic prayer, a prayer of thanksgiving and sanctification. The priest invites the people to lift up their hearts to the Lord in prayer and thanks; he unites them with himself in the prayer he addresses in their name to the Father through Jesus Christ. The meaning of the prayer is that the entire congregation joins itself to Christ in acknowledging the great things God has done and GIRM, 54 *in offering the sacrifice.*

From these principles flow consequences that concern the singing done at this time:

1. Of all the times in the Mass it is at the eucharistic prayer understood as "proclamation of the marvels of God" and "a sacrifice of praise" that singing should be highlighted and show off its celebratory value to the fullest.

2. The eucharistic prayer is an action of the "entire assembly of the faithful." Singing is the best means for emphasizing this.

Articulated at four distinct moments

The ritual indicates four moments of the eucharistic prayer as moments for singing:

1. At the opening: the INITIAL DIALOGUE between the one presiding and the entire assembly.

2. At the passage leading from the preface, the ACCLAMATION OF THE SANCTUS.

3. At the climactic moment—the memorial ("anamnesis") of the death and resurrection of the Savior, the ACCLAMATION OF THE ANAMNESIS.

4. At the conclusion "Through him, with him, in him" with the solemn AMEN.

These are four brief insertions in the eucharistic prayer. It is not very much by comparison with the long discourse of the priest. All the more reason for giving them all their meaning and value.

The initial dialogue

The priest invites the people to lift up their hearts to the Lord in prayer and thanks; he unites them with himself in the prayer he addresses in their name to the Father through Jesus Christ.

GIRM, 54

In the name of all the baptized present, the presiding minister says: "We give thanks, we offer, we pray." How are these words going to be expressed and lived? Liturgical realities only exist if they are signified.

—By means of a dialogue in which the presiding minister arouses and starts the assembly on its way; so the assembly enters into the action and becomes a support to the celebrant who goes on in the preface ("public proclamation") to sing the marvels of God's love for humanity.

1. Is a simple recitation of the words of the dialogue sufficient to bring the assembly to a state of praise?

to raise it up: "let us lift up our hearts?" to so stimulate the group that its grateful admiration soon bursts forth in the *Sanctus*? Isn't it incongruous to say: "Lift up . . . let us give thanks . . . it is right!" in a flat, banal tone of voice?

2. It is heartrending to see so many capable priests and so many assemblies forego the singing of this dialogue. They thus deprive themselves of an ordinary way (one that is so expressive if done in a life-giving manner) "of entering together into an act of thanksgiving."

3. This is another case of one of the simple basic elements of the rite not being lived out in the liturgy.

The Sanctus

In the preface, the principal moment of thanksgiving, the priest in the name of all the holy people, glorifies God the Father. Then joining with the angels the congregation sings or recites the Sanctus. This acclamation is an intrinsic part of the eucharistic prayer.

GIRM, 55

The praise given is no longer only that of the priest nor of the people assembled but of all creation visible and invisible addressed to the "God of the universe" because of "He who comes."

1. When the priest ends the preface saying: "as we sing," the whole assembly, hanging on his words, should immediately exclaim: "Holy, holy...." There is nothing more disastrous than the hesitation, the wait caused by the intonation of the organ that does not come or that delays in coming; the hesitation of the leader, the technical worries of the choral

leader.... A clear note from the organ or the director should be enough.

2. The singing of the *Sanctus* is performed more effectively and is more understandable if after an initial sung dialogue, the celebrant chants the preface—on condition of course that he does it in a lively, authentic style and if the *Sanctus* picks up directly from the final phrases, which should be written with a sustained, connective cadence.

3. We might also seek alternate texts appropriately reflecting the sacred adoration of the Seraphim recounted in Isaiah.

4. Finally, we recommend a "Holy" that all language groups can learn and sing together. In the United States, the Vermulst *Holy* seems to be developing in this direction.

The Anamnesis

The Vatican II reforms introduced into the Roman liturgy after the Institution narrative an acclamation of the people which is found in all eastern liturgies. This acclamation echoes the words of the presider (or anticipates them) which proclaim what the eucharistic meal brings about: the death and resurrection of the Lord until he comes. It is an important moment.

1. While the priest addresses God the Father, the assembly addresses itself to Christ himself by acclaiming: "Dying you destroyed our death..." without excluding the third person: "Christ has died."

2. The progression is more readily felt and understood when (as is done in the children's eucharistic

prayers) this acclamation is placed after the *anamnesis* prayer offered by the celebrant.

Final doxology

The eucharistic prayer, which began with an act of praise, will end in praise by means of a "doxology" (a formula for praise).

GIRM, 55

...the praise of God is expressed in the doxology to which the people's acclamation is an assent and a conclusion.

1. Normally the presider—with the other priests— intones: "Through him, with him" which flows into the simple *Amen* (sol-la) or the solemn *Amen* (sol-mi-sol-la-do-si-la) of the people. N.B.—We consider it a waste of time to upset the assemblies that are now peacefully into the habit of also singing the "through him. . ." with the priest.

2. A simple *Amen* often cannot convincingly conclude the whole eucharistic prayer and express the acceptance of the New Covenant. This has brought about new research, culminating in the triple *Amen* (sung straight through or mingled with the "through him" or in the form of a canon) or really singable doxology forms such as are found in the eucharistic prayers for children.

Looked upon as a part of the total action involved in the Lord's Supper

The eucharistic prayer cannot really be understood or performed if it is not viewed in the overall reality of the Lord's Supper as we explained in Chapter 5.

1. What precedes the eucharistic prayer:

—Does the dialogue seem like a threshold, a departure, or does it occur in an insignificant chain of words?

—Has a processional or act of praise already been sung?

—Was everyone aware that a "meal" was beginning?

2. What follows the eucharistic prayer:

—How does it flow into the "Our Father"? Spoken, chanted, sung? and what follows? And its doxology?

For a more lyrical eucharistic prayer

Since Vatican II we have been fortunate in being able to be more authentically involved in the eucharistic prayer. But there are things still to be done:

—texts that are more lyrical, more poetic, more singable;

—participation by the assembly that is better integrated into the eucharistic prayer in its entirety; more unified action from the initial dialogue to the final *Amen* so that the eucharistic prayer is really the center and summit not only of the Mass but of the singing done at liturgical assemblies.

15

BEFORE COMMUNION

Points of reference

After the Lord had taken into his hand the bread or the cup (what we do at the beginning of the eucharist) after giving thanks to his Father (this corresponds to the eucharistic prayer) he shared the bread and had the cup passed around. He gave his disciples something to eat and drink, his "body and blood as spiritual food."

GIRM, 56

After the eucharistic prayer we begin the rites for communion. It is a complex series of actions with three distinct steps:

1. A preparation "before communion" with the Our Father, the sign of peace, the sharing of the bread.

2. The communion itself where each one is invited to eat and drink.

3. A period of silence, singing, and prayer after communion.

Then the rites of "sending forth."

Rites and Songs

As in other moments of the Lord's Supper, the preparation for communion that we are speaking of here loses itself in singing and music: chanting of the Our Father by all, of the "Lead us...." by the priest, of the doxology "For the Kingdom...," by all; singing at the "fraction of the bread."

Before considering each of these in itself, I would like to make two general remarks:

1. If the eucharistic prayer has been well celebrated, it has been the climax of the entire celebration and—let us at least suppose—a singing "climax." The moment of communion will soon constitute another "climax" for each person present: that of his or her personal sacramental participation in the mystery of the Body of Christ. But the celebration cannot move along solely by progressing from climax to climax. Its progress is cadenced by tension and release, by songs and silence or simple words, by major symbols and supplementary signs. It follows that even if the elements of the period before communion are valuable (the Lord's Prayer; sign of peace and sharing of the bread), considered in the overall action of the Mass, they constitute a transition leading the action to a further place. Except for certain allowances for special days (e.g., a song for peace) the musical elements should not eclipse what went before or what comes after.

2. The role that furnishes the key to understanding the meaning of the rites before communion and their coherence is clearly communion itself seen as a mystery of unity. The theme that permeates these actions is reconciliation-sharing.

   According to liturgical tradition, the high point of "penitential preparation" is not at the beginning of Mass but here: "Forgive us as we forgive... Grant us peace... In your mercy keep us..." Reconciliation is effected simultaneously wth God and among ourselves. All this tends to assure the authenticity of the sharing of the bread: God shares with us; it is up to us to share....

The Lord's Prayer

Here we ask for today's bread (the bread of the day of the Lord) and pardon for our offenses.

It is a prayer not really a song. And it is a common prayer: "Let us pray: Our Father...."

After the doxology "through him" and the *Amen* that concludes the great prayer of praise, there is some important punctuation. After the great public act of praise, there comes a more intimate prayer. Having prayer upon prayer (eucharistic prayer + the Our Father) does not make the observance of this punctuation any easier. We have reason to lament the absence of the ancient order preserved in Milan and in Egypt where the fraction (a gesture) follows the eucharistic prayer. Then comes the Our Father in a place more closely linked to communion. In our circumstances we can at least change the "tone" of our participation. That is why an Our Father recited by all slowly, quietly, dwelling on the words, is often the most meaningful and appropriate manner of saying it.

It is essential to teach our assemblies to say the Our Father slowly and meditatively. The effect of this practice comes as a discovery and surprise to many. But since the pull of old habits tends to make the recitation mechanical, we will have to remind our assemblies periodically: slowly, quietly, etc.

However, chanting remains an ordinary way to offer common prayer. It differs from singing in that the melody does not predominate. The words do. Furthermore, chanting allows a homogeneous and unified progression a) from the invitation of the priest: "As Our Savior taught us...," (b) to the chanting by all, c) to the development by the priest: "Deliver us," opening on to d) the acclamation "for the Kingdom...are yours." From a celebratory point of view this is very worthwhile. It moves, develops, rests —which is appropriate for a transitional element.

In France, the official melody of the missal has not been a popular success. But when it is well executed, it is excellent and is well liked by many communities.

It is the version of the Our Father adapted from Rimsky-Korsakof which has spontaneously spread throughout our country. Its polyphony certainly accounts at least partially for its success. But its melody and recitative style fall right into the tradition and spirit of the chant—provided that the chanting retains a light tone and does not dissolve into romantic pathos or rhythmic weakness.

Among the other Our Fathers, priority, at least in reference to the Mass, should be given to those which interiorize the text rather than to those which make a "song" of it.

For yours is the Kingdom...

In the French missal two versions of this doxology have been provided for concluding the section on the Lord's Prayer. One to be said ("For to you belong..."); the other to be sung ("For to you the Kingdom...").

It is too bad that this doxology is so rarely sung. The music (in the missal) is very well done, with popular appeal and musicality if the rhythm is respected. It could be sung even if what preceded it was recited for some good reason. Doing it this way gives breathing space during the celebration and relaxes people before the sign of peace.

The prayer for peace and the sign of peace

Here neither singing nor music are suggested. That is a good idea, because in a moment the singing for the sharing of the bread will begin. Nevertheless:

a) In certain circumstances when one wishes to give a special meaning to the sign of peace (reconciliation day, special gathering, etc.), a song may accompany this sign. (Another one is not added at the fraction; but the two can be combined as in Tom Parker's "Peace I leave with you/Lamb of God").

b) In large churches and assemblies during the sign of peace, a gentle organ background or music of some kind, such as a prelude to the song for the sharing of the bread, could be attractive.

The song for the sharing of the bread

The sign of the breaking of the bread exists not only as a constituent rite of the Christian eucharist, but remains a most telling, always current, universal symbol.

We must deplore the almost non-existence of this symbolic sign in the great majority of parish eucharists. But this is not the appropriate place to show how to give it more importance. Let us merely indicate that this sign does not consist only of breaking the host or cutting a loaf of bread into pieces. There is the further arrangement of the pieces on the plates and the involvement of the ministers of communion from this time on. Briefly, all that shows we are moving out from a single loaf of bread toward all our table companions.

A song accompanies this rite. In the Roman liturgy, it is traditionally a litany: "Lamb of God who takes away the sins of the world. R—have mercy on us." The rubrics tell us:

GIRM 56e

This invocation may be repeated as often as necessary to accompany the breaking of the bread. The final reprise concludes with the words: "grant us peace." We are not tied to the triple recitation. It can be 1, 2, 3 or 10. Evidently it depends also on the music. A real litany with a simple response continues to be the most popular.

We are not limited to the words "Lamb of God" either. These words are already well represented in the Mass. In the Milanese rite the song at the breaking of the bread is a "real" song with a changing text that develops the rich significance of the mystery of communion. A song with a rich content is better recognized at this moment when the entire assembly is ready to sing than during the communion procession when one doesn't have a book and is occupied with something more important. Many of the songs traditionally identified as communion songs are enhanced by being sung at the sharing of the bread rather than during communion.

Let me make the final remark that a suitable song that is attractive and rather long can be begun during the sharing of the bread and after the invitation to communion ("Happy are those who are called..."), to be continued during the procession. Too many different songs use up a repertory and wear down the users.

16

DURING AND
AFTER COMMUNION

DURING COMMUNION

When the symbolic sharing of the bread has been completed, the president invites those present to partake of the Lord's Table. While all eat and drink, a song rises up *to express outwardly the communicants' union in spirit by means of the unity of their voices, to give evidence of joy of heart, and to make the procession to receive Christ's body more fully an act of community.*

GIRM, 56

The processional song

Although a processional movement is not obligatory or always possible, it remains the ordinary form practiced in the average assembly. This is not done only for practical reasons. The movement is full of meaning.

1. Each one comes by way of a personal approach to receive the Gift of God. The waiting in line, the outstretched hand of the child or beggar, all this bespeaks the conduct of a poor person.

2. The bread received is bread for the road. We take it as it was taken at the first Passover, hastily, dressed for travel, ready for our exodus.

3. It is a whole people on the march advancing toward

a Promised Land. The song should, therefore, have the characteristics of a "processional."

a) This procession differs from the others (beginning of Mass; offertory procession) in that everyone or almost everyone takes part. No one should have to be bothered with a book or paper for singing at this time. Everyone processing should be able to join in the singing easily, if they so desire, e.g., by a brief refrain.

b) So that the singing can be sustained in a moving assembly where some sing and others do not (especially if they are eating or drinking), there has to be a stable, fixed support to the singing: animator-soloist, or better still a choral group that sings couplets, versicles, stanzas, with possibly an accompanying instrument that can fill in interludes and allow for some breathing space.

A joyful song

Acts 2, 41

Just as the first Christians, according to the Acts of the Apostles, "took their food with joy and simplicity of heart" in memory of the meals the Risen Jesus took in the midst of his own people, so the eucharistic communicants manifest in their singing the joy of those who were hungry and who are now satisfied. It is a very intimate joy prompted by the Spirit. But how can we fail to share it when we give it expression in song?

A song of union

Those who become one body symbolize their deep unity in the union and harmony of their voices. Singing is here, more than elsewhere, a special sign of communion and mutual love.

Some good practices...

Of all liturgical songs the communion song is one of the best known to liturgical tradition. The oft quoted text in these songs is Psalm 33: "Taste and see how good the Lord is." A good number of communion hymns have come down to us from the first centuries. The processional: "Father we thank thee who has planted" echoes one of these hymns from the Didache and is a model of this type of song.

From the beginning of the renewal of liturgical music, the communion song has been widely used and continues to be popular.

However, with the importance given to the song at the moment of "sharing" and especially the introduction of a hymn after communion, experience tends to dictate making choices. Many now prefer to sing the hymn after communion and allow the communion to proceed in silence (or against a background of instrumental music). This practice is generally accepted especially in assemblies that, because they like to sing, have already sung a great deal during the Mass, and prefer to receive communion in peace.

AFTER COMMUNION

GIRM 56j

After communion, the priest and people may spend some time in silent prayer. If desired, a hymn, psalm, or other song of praise may be sung by the entire congregation.

This innovation of Vatican II had been broadly prepared by the "songs of thanksgiving" sung after low or sung masses. It is really rather natural that the entire eucharistic action culminate in a song that could be looked upon as a finishing touch.

Anyone who has experimented with the suggestion of the new missal knows the value of a well-sung hymn after communion. There are several conditions for success:

A song which arises from silence

Real silence. A time when nothing and no one is moving about (no purification of the ciborium; no moving around; no music). Common praise will arise from the depth and intensity of this silence.

A song in unison

Of all the songs in the Mass this is the one that all present, from the presider to the late arrivals, are available to execute together and with only one activity in mind, that of singing.

A song in choral form

We are not speaking strictly of a "choral" in the absolute sense (although this is often the most appropriate form for unison singing to take) but rather in the sense that the form used should allow for the participation of all in a single choir. The versed hymn is quite appropriate here. There is no need of a refrain, a solo leader, or of a choir (though this latter could harmonize with the singing). Everyone begins singing and continues to the end. This is a very special moment in the Mass if it is well executed.

The concluding song

Evidently it is impossible to add on another concluding song. It could be justified only when nothing special could be included in the Mass. It would be a question of "making up afterwards." However, the practice of this concluding song is tenacious. After having said "Go in peace," what significance is there in doing just the opposite by detaining everyone for another song?

Nevertheless, it is reasonable to enrich the ritual "Thanks be to God" by repeating a refrain-acclamation that had pertinent meaning during the celebration and makes a good "sending forth."

The normal order of the celebration should be: end of communion, silence, song, prayer after communion. Then: the announcements, the blessing, the sending forth. But there is a problem with the series of postures required. If you have just stood for the prayer after communion, you have to sit down again for the announcements and get up for the blessing (because people standing up and ready to go do not hear the announcements). That causes a lot of unappreciated standing up and sitting down. Therefore, since most of the thanksgiving songs are well sung when people are seated, and as a prolongation of silence, it might be well to attach the announcements here, and then, once the people are standing, to link the prayer after communion to the sending forth.

SELECTIONS FROM THE GENERAL INSTRUCTION OF THE ROMAN MISSAL

N.B. Many times during the course of the preceding pages we have quoted GIRM, *The General Instruction of the Roman Missal.* All the rules for celebration and the meaning of all the rites are found there. It is the basic text for all who are responsible for liturgy, and may be found in the opening pages of all altar missals. The most important section of Chapter II is given here.

The Structure, Elements, and Parts of the Mass

I: GENERAL STRUCTURE OF THE MASS

7. At Mass or the Lord's Supper, the people of God are called together, with a priest presiding and acting in the person of Christ, to celebrate the memorial of the Lord or eucharistic sacrifice. For this reason Christ's promise applies supremely to such a local gathering together of the Church: "Where two or three come together in my name, there am I in their midst" (Matt. 18:20).

8. The Mass is made up as it were of the liturgy of the word and the liturgy of the eucharist, two parts so closely connected that they form but one single act of worship. For in the Mass the table of God's word and of Christ's body is laid for the people of God to receive from it instruction and food. There are also certain rites to open and conclude the celebration.

III: INDIVIDUAL PARTS OF THE MASS

A. INTRODUCTORY RITES

24. The parts preceding the liturgy of the word, namely, the entrance song, greeting, penitential rite, *Kyrie, Gloria,* and open-

ing prayer or collect, have the character of a beginning, introduction, and preparation.

The purpose of these rites is that the faithful coming together take on the form of a community and prepare themselves to listen to God's word and celebrate the eucharist properly.

Entrance

25. After the people have assembled, the entrance song begins as the priest and the ministers come in. The purpose of this song is to open the celebration, intensify the unity of the gathered people, lead their thoughts to the mystery of the season or feast, and accompany the procession of priest and ministers.

26. The entrance song is sung alternately either by the choir and the congregation or by the cantor and the congregation; or it is sung entirely by the congregation or by the choir alone. The antiphon and psalm of the Graduale Romanum or The Simple Gradual may be used, or another song that is suited to this part of the Mass, the day, or the season and that has a text approved by the conference of bishops.

If there is no singing for the entrance, the antiphon in the Missal is recited either by the faithful, by some of them, or by a reader; otherwise it is recited by the priest after the greeting.

Veneration of the altar and greeting of the congregation

27. When the priest and the ministers enter the sanctuary, they reverence the altar. As a sign of veneration, the priest and deacon kiss the altar; when the occasion warrants, the priest may also incense the altar.

28. After the entrance song, the priest and the whole assembly make the sign of the cross. Then through his greeting the priest declares to the assembled community that the Lord is present. This greeting and the congregation's response express the mystery of the gathered Church.

Penitential rite

29. After greeting the congregation, the priest or other qualified minister may very briefly introduce the faithful to the Mass of the day. Then the priest invites them to take part in the penitential rite, which the entire community carries out

through a communal confession and which the priest's absolution brings to an end.

Kyrie eleison

30. Then the *Kyrie* begins, unless it has already been included as part of the penitential rite. Since it is a song by which the faithful praise the Lord and implore his mercy, it is ordinarily prayed by all, that is, alternately by the congregation and the choir or cantor.

   As a rule each of the acclamations is said twice, but, because of the idiom of different languages, the music, or other circumstances, it may be said more than twice or a short verse (trope) may be interpolated. If the *Kyrie* is not sung, it is to be recited.

Gloria

31. The *Gloria* is an ancient hymn in which the Church, assembled in the Holy Spirit, praises and entreats the Father and the Lamb. It is sung by the congregation, or by the congregation alternately with the choir, or by the choir alone. If not sung, it is to be recited either by all together or in alternation.

   The *Gloria* is sung or said on Sundays outside Advent and Lent, on solemnities and feasts, and in special, more solemn celebrations.

Opening prayer or collect

32. Next the priest invites the people to pray and together with him they observe a brief silence so that they may realize they are in God's presence and may call their petitions to mind. The priest then says the opening prayer, which custom has named the "collect." This expresses the theme of the celebration and the priest's words address a petition to God the Father through Christ in the Holy Spirit.

   The people make the prayer their own and give their assent by the acclamation, *Amen....*

B. LITURGY OF THE WORD

33. Readings from Scripture and the chants between the readings form the main part of the liturgy of the word. The homily,

profession of faith, and general intercessions or prayer of the faithful expand and complete this part of the Mass. In the readings, explained by the homily, God is speaking to his people, opening up to them the mystery of redemption and salvation, and nourishing their spirit; Christ is present to the faithful through his own word. Through the chants the people make God's word their own and through the profession of faith affirm their adherence to it. Finally, having been fed by this word, they make their petitions in the general intercessions for the needs of the Church and for the salvation of the whole world.

Scripture readings

34. The readings lay the table of God's word for the faithful and open up the riches of the Bible to them. Since by tradition the reading of the Scriptures is a ministerial, not a presidential function, it is proper that as a rule a deacon or, in his absence, a priest other than the one presiding read the gospel.
A reader proclaims the other readings. In the absence of a deacon or another priest, the priest celebrant reads the gospel.

35. The liturgy itself inculcates the great reverence to be shown toward the reading of the gospel, setting it off from the other readings by special marks of honor. A special minister is appointed to proclaim it and prepares himself by a blessing or prayer. The people, who by their acclamations acknowledge and confess Christ present and speaking to them, stand as they listen to it. Marks of reverence are given to the Book of the Gospels itself.

Chants between the readings

36. After the first reading comes the responsorial psalm or gradual, an integral part of the liturgy of the word. The psalm as a rule is drawn from the Lectionary because the individual psalm texts are directly connected with the individual readings: the choice of psalm depends therefore on the readings. Nevertheless, in order that the people may be able to join in the responsorial psalm more readily, some texts of responses and psalms have been chosen, according to the different seasons of the year and classes of saints, for optional use, whenever the psalm is sung, in place of the text corresponding to the reading.

The psalmist or cantor of the psalm sings the verses of the psalm at the lectern or other suitable place. The people remain seated and listen, but also as a rule take part by singing the response, except when the psalm is sung straight through without the response.

The psalm when sung may be either the psalm assigned in the Lectionary or the gradual from the *Graduale Romanum* or the responsorial psalm or the psalm with *Alleluia* as the response from the *The Simple Gradual* in the form they have in those books.

37. As the season requires, the *Alleluia* or another chant follows the second reading.

    a. The *Alleluia* is sung in every season outside Lent. It is begun either by all present or by the choir or cantor; it may then be repeated. The verses are taken from the Lectionary or the *Graduale*.

    b. The other chant consists of the verse before the gospel or another psalm or tract, as found in the Lectionary or the *Graduale*.

38. When there is only one reading before the gospel:

    a. during a season calling for the *Alleluia*, there is an option to use either the psalm with *Alleluia* as the response, or the responsorial psalm and the *Alleluia* with its verse, or just the psalm, or just the *Alleluia*;

    b. during the season when the *Alleluia* is not allowed, either the responsorial psalm or the verse before the gospel may be used.

39. If the psalm after the reading is not sung, it is to be recited. If not sung, the *Alleluia* or the verse before the gospel may be omitted.

40. Sequences are optional, except on Easter Sunday and Pentecost.

Homily

41. The homily is an integral part of the liturgy and is strongly recommended: it is necessary for the nurturing of the Christian life. It should develop some point of the readings or of

another text from the Ordinary or from the Proper of the Mass of the day, and take into account the mystery being celebrated and the needs proper to the listeners.

42. There must be a homily on Sundays and holydays of obligation at all Masses that are celebrated with a congregation. It is recommended on other days, especially on the weekdays of Advent, Lent, and the Easter season, as well as on other feasts and occasions when the people come to church in large numbers.

Profession of Faith

43. The symbol or profession of faith in the celebration of Mass serves as a way for the people to respond and to give their assent to the word of God heard in the readings and through the homily and for them to call to mind the truths of faith before they begin to celebrate the eucharist.

45. Recitation of the profession of faith by the priest together with the people is obligatory on Sundays and solemnities. It may be said also at special, more solemn celebrations.

If it is sung, as a rule all are to sing it together or in alternation.

General Intercessions

45. In the general intercessions or prayer of the faithful, the people, exercising their priestly function, intercede for all humanity. It is appropriate that this prayer be included in all Masses celebrated with a congregation, so that petitions will be offered for the Church, for civil authorities, for those oppressed by various needs, for all people, and for the salvation of the world.

46. As a rule the sequence of intentions is to be:

a. for the needs of the Church;
b. for public authorities and the salvation of the world;
c. for those oppressed by any need;
d. for the local community.

In particular celebrations, such as confirmations, marriages, funerals, etc., the series of intercessions may refer more specifically to the occasion.

47. It belongs to the priest celebrant to direct the general intercessions, by means of a brief introduction to invite the congregation to pray, and after the intercessions to say the concluding prayer. It is desirable that a deacon, cantor, or other person announce the intentions. The whole assembly gives expression to its supplication either by a response said together after each intention or by silent prayer.

C. LITURGY OF THE EUCHARIST

48. At the last supper Christ instituted the sacrifice and paschal meal that make the sacrifice of the cross to be continuously present in the Church, when the priest, representing Christ the Lord, carries out what the Lord did and handed over to his disciples to do in his memory.

   Christ took the bread and the cup and gave thanks; he broke the bread and gave it to his disciples, saying: "Take and eat, this is my body." Giving the cup, he said: "Take and drink, this is the cup of my blood. Do this in memory of me." Accordingly, the Church has planned the celebration of the eucharistic liturgy around the parts corresponding to these words and actions of Christ:

   1. In the preparation of the gifts, the bread and the wine with water are brought to the altar, that is, the same elements that Christ used.

   2. In the eucharistic prayer thanks is given to God for the whole work of salvation and the gifts of bread and wine become the body and blood of Christ.

   3. Through the breaking of the one bread the unity of the faithful is expressed and through communion they receive the Lord's body and blood in the same way the apostles received them from Christ's own hands.

Preparation of the gifts

49. At the beginning of the liturgy of the eucharist the gifts, which will become Christ's body and blood, are brought to the altar.

   First the altar, the Lord's table, which is the center of the whole eucharistic liturgy, is prepared: the corporal, purificator, missal, and chalice are placed on it (unless the chalice is prepared at a side table).

The gifts are then brought forward. It is desirable for the faithful to present the bread and wine, which are accepted by the priest or deacon at a convenient place. The gifts are placed on the altar to the accompaniment of the prescribed texts. Even though the faithful no longer, as in the past, bring the bread and wine for the liturgy from their homes, the rite of carrying up the gifts retains the same spiritual value and meaning.

This is also the time to receive money or other gifts for the church or the poor brought by the faithful or collected at the Mass. These are to be put in a suitable place but not on the altar.

50. The procession bringing the gifts is accompanied by the presentation song, which continues at least until the gifts have been placed on the altar. The rules for this song are the same as those for the entrance song (no. 26). If it is not sung, the presentation antiphon is omitted.

51. The gifts on the altar and the altar itself may be incensed. This is a symbol of the Church's offering and prayer going up to God. Afterward the deacon or other minister may incense the priest and the people.

52. The priest then washes his hands as an expression of his desire to be cleansed within.

53. Once the gifts have been placed on the altar and the accompanying rites completed, the preparation of the gifts comes to an end through the invitation to pray with the priest and the prayer over the gifts, which are a preparation for the eucharistic prayer.

Eucharistic prayer

54. Now the center and summit of the entire celebration begins: the eucharistic prayer, a prayer of thanksgiving and sanctification. The priest invites the people to lift up their hearts to the Lord in prayer and thanks; he unites them with himself in the prayer he addresses in their name to the Father through Jesus Christ. The meaning of the prayer is that the entire congregation joins itself to Christ in acknowledging the great things God has done and in offering the sacrifice.

55. The chief elements making up the eucharistic prayer are these:

a. Thanksgiving (expressed especially in the preface): in the name of the entire people of God, the priest praises the Father and gives thanks to him for the whole work of salvation or for some special aspect of it that corresponds to the day, feast, or season.

b. Acclamation: joining with the angels, the congregation sings or recites the Sanctus. This acclamation is an intrinsic part of the eucharistic prayer and all the people join with the priest in singing or reciting it.

c. Epiclesis: in special invocations the Church calls on God's power and asks that the gifts offered by human hands be consecrated, that is, become Christ's body and blood, and that the victim to be received in communion be the source of salvation for those who will partake.

d. Institution narrative and consecration: in the words and actions of Christ, that sacrifice is celebrated which he himself instituted at the Last Supper, when, under the appearances of bread and wine, he offered his body and blood, gave them to his apostles to eat and drink, then commanded that they carry on this mystery.

e. Anamnesis: in fulfillment of the command received from Christ through the apostles, the Church keeps his memorial by recalling especially his passion, resurrection, and ascension.

f. Offering: in this memorial, the Church—and in particular the Church here and now assembled—offers the spotless victim to the Father in the Holy Spirit. The Church's intention is that the faithful not only offer this victim but also learn to offer themselves and so to surrender themselves, through Christ the Mediator, to an ever more complete union with the Father and with each other, so that at last God may be all in all.

g. Intercessions: the intercessions make it clear that the eucharist is celebrated in communion with the entire Church of heaven and earth and that the offering is made for the Church and all its members, living and dead, who are called to share in the salvation and redemption purchased by Christ's body and blood.

h. Final doxology: the praise of God is expressed in the doxology, to which the people's acclamation is an assent and a conclusion.

The eucharistic prayer calls for all to listen in silent reverence, but also to take part through the acclamations for which the rite makes provision.

Communion Rite

56. Since the eucharistic celebration is the paschal meal, it is right that the faithful who are properly disposed receive the Lord's body and blood as spiritual food as he commanded. This is the purpose of the breaking of bread and the other preparatory rites that lead directly to the communion of the people:

a. Lord's Prayer: this is a petition both for daily food, which for Christians means also the eucharistic bread, and for the forgiveness of sin, so that what is holy may be given to those who are holy. The priest offers the invitation to pray, but all the faithful say the prayer with him; he alone adds the embolism, *Deliver us*, which the people conclude with a doxology. The embolism, developing the last petition of the Lord's Prayer, begs on behalf of the entire community of the faithful deliverance from the power of evil. The invitation, the prayer itself, the embolism, and the people's doxology are sung or are recited aloud.

b. Rite of peace: before they share in the same bread, the faithful implore peace and unity for the Church and for the whole human family and offer some sign of their love for one another.

The form the sign of peace should take is left to the conference of bishops to determine, in accord with the culture and customs of the people.

c. Breaking of the bread: in apostolic times this gesture of Christ at the last supper gave the entire eucharistic action its name. This rite is not simply functional, but is a sign that in sharing in the one bread of life which is Christ we who are many are made one body (see 1 Cor 10:17).

d. Commingling: the celebrant drops a part of the host into the chalice.

e. *Agnus Dei*: during the breaking of the bread and the commingling, the *Agnus Dei* is as a rule sung by the choir or cantor with the congregation responding; otherwise it is recited aloud. This invocation may be repeated as often as necessary to accompany the breaking of the bread. The final reprise concludes with the words, *grant us peace*.

f. Personal preparation of the priest: the priest prepares himself by the prayer, said softly, that he may receive Christ's body and blood to good effect. The faithful do the same by silent prayer.

g. The priest then shows the eucharistic bread for communion to the faithful and with them recites the prayer of humility in words from the Gospels.

h. It is most desirable that the faithful receive the Lord's body from hosts consecrated at the same Mass and that, in the instances when it is permitted, they share in the chalice. Then even through the signs communion will stand out more clearly as a sharing in the sacrifice actually being celebrated.

i. During the priest's and faithful's reception of the sacrament the communion song is sung. Its function is to express outwardly the communicants' union in spirit by means of the unity of their voices, to give evidence of joy of heart, and to make the procession to receive Christ's body more fully an act of community. The song begins when the priest takes communion and continues for as long as seems appropriate while the faithful receive Christ's body. But the communion song should be ended in good time whenever there is to be a hymn after communion.

An antiphon from the *Graduale Romanum* may also be used with or without the psalm, or an antiphon with psalm from *The Simple Gradual* or another suitable song approved by the conference of bishops. It is sung by the choir alone or by the choir or cantor with the congregation.

If there is no singing, the communion antiphon in the Missal is recited either by the people, by some of them, or by a reader. Otherwise the priest himself says it after he has received communion and before he gives communion to the faithful.

j. After communion, the priest and people may spend some time in silent prayer. If desired, a hymn, psalm, or other song of praise may be sung by the entire congregation.

k. In the prayer after communion, the priest petitions for the effects of the mystery just celebrated and by their acclamation, *Amen*, the people make the prayer their own.

D. CONCLUDING RITE

57. The concluding rite consists of:

a. The priest's greeting and blessing, which on certain days and occasions is expanded and expressed in the prayer over the people or another more solemn formulary:

b. the dismissal of the assembly, which sends each member back to doing good works, while praising and blessing the Lord.